QUICK VEGETARIAN PLEASURES

To Liz,
all the best,

Jeanne Lemlin
3·28·92

Happy Birthday!

Also by Jeanne Lemlin

Vegetarian Pleasures: A Menu Cookbook

Quick

VEGETARIAN PLEASURES

Jeanne Lemlin

HarperPerennial

A Division of HarperCollinsPublishers

HarperCollins books may be purchased for educational, business, or sales promotional use. For information, please call or write: Special Markets Department, HarperCollinsPublishers, Inc., 10 East 53rd Street, New York, NY 10022. Telephone: (212) 207-7528; Fax: (212) 207-7222.

FIRST EDITION

Designed by
Stephanie Tevonian

Library of Congress Cataloging-in-Publication Data
Lemlin, Jeanne.
   Quick vegetarian pleasures / Jeanne Lemlin.
     p. cm.
  ISBN 0-06-055324-3 — ISBN 0-06-096911-3 (pbk.)
   1. Vegetarian cookery. 2. Quick and easy cookery. I. Title.
TX832.L46 1992
641.5′636—dc20   91-50515
92 93 94 95 96 RRD 10 9 8 7 6 5 4 3 2 1
92 93 94 95 96 RRD 10 9 8 7 6 5 4 3 2 1 (pbk.)

To my husband, Ed, whose unending help with typing, grocery shopping, dishwashing, and the care of our son, allowed me to write this book

and

to my mother, who let me, from a very early age, totally overrun her kitchen.

CONTENTS

INTRODUCTION

Shortly after the publication of my first book, Vegetarian Pleasures: A Menu Cookbook, *my son Daniel was born. His wondrous arrival precipitated a host of changes in our household, the way only an infant can turn your life upside down. Some of these changes I was prepared for; others were completely unexpected.*

I had always taken for granted my habit of spending long hours in the kitchen experimenting with new foods and recipes. The more complex and time-consuming a task was, the more I would be drawn to it. No matter how busy my day, I would find myself inexorably gravitating toward the kitchen to seek some new culinary challenge. This all came to an abrupt halt. Although my love of cooking has continued unabated, I now wish to create only dishes that can be assembled quickly. If a recipe looks like it might take more than thirty minutes of my time, I lose all interest. Quickness has gained a whole new appeal.

Many people think of vegetarian cooking as being more time-consuming than traditional fare. In many cases it is. But I knew from developing a chapter on quick menus in Vegetarian Pleasures: A Menu Cookbook *that, with a good dose of imagination, meatless cooking can be fast and easy. Without sacrificing quality for convenience, I have been able to wed my love of adventurous eating with speed in the kitchen. An abundant use of fresh vegetables, grains, herbs, semi-exotic ingredients, and new items on the market still are the staples of my cooking, but I have learned to handle them with a quick hand.*

Some ready-made products have found their way into my repertoire, but none at the expense of flavor. For example, I searched for and found a commercial tomato sauce that I like, and I can spruce it up with red wine, herbs, and garlic if I desire. Salsa is another store-bought item that can vary greatly by brand, and I have found some exceptionally good ones that free me from concocting my own in the kitchen. And canned cooked beans have more often than not replaced freshly cooked dried beans in my meal planning, enabling me to incorporate more beans in my diet. Many canned beans contain a preservative — their one drawback — but I avoid preservatives in most other foods, so I allow myself this shortcut. Again, brands vary, so I have searched for and found a product with firm beans, and I always rinse them thoroughly before using them in a recipe.

My idea of a quick recipe is one that takes less than thirty minutes to prepare, though it might demand additional cooking time. If a soup has to simmer one hour on the stove, I overlook that time because I don't have to tend to the soup. Many recipes, such as Capellini with Tomato Pesto (page 116), take just ten minutes to prepare, and they taste as wonderful as many more-involved dishes. If the quality of ingredients is high, I have found, then elaborate preparations aren't necessary for noteworthy results. (Incidentally, the length of recipe directions is not necessarily an indication of the time needed to prepare a dish. Detailed instructions are a reflection of my background as a cooking instructor and my desire to be precise rather than a measure of how involved a particular recipe is.)

Although I am a vegetarian and convinced of the link between diet and health, I have always tried to maintain a relaxed stance toward meal planning. When meat is removed from our diets, we must find other sources such as beans, grains, dairy products, and soy foods to replace the lost protein and iron. And it is not only essential to eat a lot of these important foods, but also to seek variety in our diets.

But I don't believe in meticulously calculating nutritional needs and planning our meals according to these calculations. I think this approach to eating hampers pleasure at the table, and pleasure is what good eating is all about. Once eating is turned into a mathematics problem, then drudgery sets in. (Of course, there are people who, for extreme health reasons, must be very calculating about their diets. But these are special cases that require medical guidance.)

I also maintain this approach to the amount of fat in my diet. It is very important to avoid the misconception that fat intake is not a concern for vegetarians because meat is missing from our diets and we therefore can consume all the dairy products we want. We still must restrict our use of cream, milk, cheese, and eggs because of their unusually high fat content.

Rather than try to meet a set of exact dietary guidelines, I prefer to alternate richer meals with lighter meals, making lighter dishes a more frequent part of my diet. I have found that whenever I take an extreme approach to eating, there is a backlash. If I eat very light meals for too long a period of time, I inevitably crave an ultrarich dessert as compensation (like those outrageously good Häagen-Dazs hot fudge sundaes served at our local drugstore!). So moderation is also a sensible approach to take with menu planning. If a particular entrée appeals to you and it is on the rich side, choose a light accompaniment and dessert to maintain a balance.

This relaxed yet thoughtful approach to diet might sound slack to some readers, but I am not encouraging negligence. It's just that too often health-conscious people turn eating into a regimen, and because eating then loses much of its appeal, the rigid approach soon gets dropped in search of a new routine.

The general guidelines that I follow are to seek protein complementarity, restrict fats and sugar, and include a wide variety of high-fiber foods. (Protein complementarity means combining different nonmeat sources of protein in the same meal to make them complete, thereby enhancing their quality and accessibility. The foods that best complement each other are: grains and legumes; grains and dairy products; and seeds and legumes.) By keeping these basic principles in mind, I can balance my diet in an easygoing manner. Rather than make each meal a model of nutritional perfection, I can remember which foods I should include—and do so often but not always.

We should be informed about nutrition, strive to eat sensibly, and be concerned about our health. But eating must not become a religion; that's no way to feed our souls. Instead, let's approach eating with a cautious but relaxed spirit. I hope these recipes enable you to prepare delectable food in a short time and inspire you to be adventurous. Above all, I hope they enhance your cooking pleasures, quick though they may be.

TIPS FOR THE BUSY COOK

☞ Whenever you prepare rice or pasta, cook an extra batch. Chill, tossing pasta with a little oil beforehand. Use in stir-fried or skillet dishes; marinate as a salad; or sprinkle with a few tablespoons of water, cover with foil, and reheat in the oven.

☞ On weekends, make an extra-large pot of soup. Doubling a recipe doesn't mean double work. Undercook the soup, then spoon out a portion to serve later in the week or freeze a batch.

☞ Don't shy away from recipes that serve six, even though there may be just one or two people in your household. Leftovers are the salvation of the busy person.

☞ Keep your pantry and refrigerator well stocked. It's easier to assemble a quick meal if you've got plenty of ingredients on hand.

☞ Go out to dinner.

APPETIZERS

*A*ppetizers play a special role in menu planning, especially when you are entertaining and want to stimulate guests' appetites with an intriguing prelude to the meal. Presenting a tempting hors d'oeuvre before your guests sit down to dinner can set the tone for the evening while enabling them to nibble while conversing. But these dishes need not be reserved for entertaining. Many are simple enough to put together quickly to precede an informal family dinner. Whether the occasion is special or not, the same rules for selection should be taken into account. If your main course contains cheese or is on the rich side, select a dairy free appetizer such as *Marinated Roasted Peppers* (page 14) or *Spicy Mixed Nuts* (page 11). If you are serving a meal free of dairy products or on the light side, then a cheesy appetizer beforehand would strike a nice balance. Hors d'oeuvres should awaken, not satisfy, the appetite, so small portions suffice.

Everyone enjoys a party in

which there is a large assortment of appetizers artfully laid out on a table. For the cook, this can be a somewhat relaxed approach to entertaining because so much of the work can be done in advance. Strive for contrasting flavors, textures, and colors to provide a tantalizing selection (see Appetizer Party menu, page 238).

CHÈVRE TOASTS WITH ASSORTED TOPPINGS

These are richly flavored and irresistible with wine. A great appetizer for a special or simple meal.

12 thin slices narrow-loaf French bread

Olive oil

¼ pound chèvre (goat cheese)

ASSORTED TOPPINGS

Marinated roasted red peppers (page 14, or use store-bought)

Capers

Black olives (preferably small, oil-cured)

Chopped fresh herbs

Cherry tomato slices

Makes 1 dozen toasts

❶ Place the bread on a baking sheet and broil on both sides until golden and crisp.

❷ Remove from the oven. Using a pastry brush, coat 1 side of each slice with some olive oil. Spread some chèvre on top of each slice, then garnish with your choice of toppings. Here are some suggestions: marinated roasted red peppers cut into strips, rolled, and placed in the center; 3 capers placed in the center; a whole black olive with a sprig of a fresh herb such as dill or parsley; overlapping cherry tomato slices; chopped fresh herbs such as chives, thyme, parsley, dill, or chervil.

CRISPY GARLIC TOASTS
(CROSTINI)

Here is one case in which garlic powder works better than fresh garlic. These toasts are light and buttery, with an assertive garlic flavor. Serve them with soup or relish them as an appetizer.

1 narrow loaf French bread
(about ½ pound)

½ cup olive oil

Garlic powder

Salt

Makes about 40 toasts

❶ Preheat the oven to 350°F. Cut the French bread into ¼- to ½-inch-thick slices. With a pastry brush, lightly coat each slice on both sides with olive oil and lay it on a baking sheet.

❷ Generously sprinkle garlic powder on top of each slice, then lightly season with some salt.

❸ Bake 5 to 7 minutes, or until *bottoms* are lightly golden. Turn the slices over and sprinkle again with garlic powder and salt. Bake 5 minutes more, or until golden all over.

❹ Place the baking sheet on a wire rack and let the toasts cool completely, about 30 minutes. Store in a covered tin or plastic bag at room temperature for up to 1 week, or freeze for up to 2 weeks.

HERB CHEESE TOASTS
(CROSTINI)

It's best to let these toasts sit for twenty-four hours before serving, to let the wonderful mingling of flavors develop fully. Also, dried herbs work better than fresh in this recipe.

1 narrow loaf French bread (about ½ pound), *or* grinder rolls

½ cup olive oil

2 tablespoons grated Parmesan cheese

½ teaspoon dried oregano

½ teaspoon dried basil

½ teaspoon dried dill

¼ teaspoon dried thyme

Makes about 40 toasts

❶ Preheat the oven to 350°F. Cut the French bread into ¼-inch-thick slices. With a pastry brush, lightly and evenly coat both sides of each slice with olive oil, then lay the slices on a baking sheet. Bake 5 minutes, then remove from the oven. Turn each slice over.

❷ In a small bowl combine the cheese with the herbs. Sprinkle the mixture evenly on top of each toast, then press down lightly with your fingertips to help stick it to the bread. Return to the oven and bake 7 to 10 minutes more, or until the cheese is golden brown and the toasts appear crisp (they will harden more upon cooling). Be careful not to burn the toasts. Cool completely on a wire rack. Store in a covered tin or plastic bag at room temperature for up to 3 days, or refrigerate up to 1 week, or freeze up to 2 weeks.

STUFFED CHERRY TOMATOES

hese little tomato cups stuffed with a ricotta cheese–scallion mixture are pretty enough for an elegant party, yet simple enough for an informal occasion.

½ cup ricotta cheese (preferably part skim)

2 tablespoons grated Parmesan cheese

1½ tablespoons very thinly sliced scallions

Freshly ground black pepper to taste

20 to 25 cherry tomatoes, stems removed

2 teaspoons minced scallions (green parts only)

Fresh parsley sprigs

Makes 20 to 25

❶ In a small bowl, beat together the ricotta and Parmesan cheeses, sliced scallions, and pepper. Cover and chill while preparing the tomato cups.

❷ Slice off ¼ of the bottom of a tomato (it will sit more securely on its stem end). With the tip of a knife, scoop out the pulp and gently squeeze out the seeds and juice. Discard the sliced-off cap, juice, and seeds. Repeat with the remaining tomatoes.

❸ Using the handle of a teaspoon, stuff each tomato with some of the ricotta mixture. To garnish, sprinkle a few minced scallion pieces on top of each tomato. Chill the tomatoes at least 30 minutes so the flavors can blend, then let sit at room temperature for 20 minutes or so before serving (cold tomatoes lose their flavor). For a striking presentation, serve on an attractive platter and garnish with bunches of parsley sprigs.

CHEESE CRACKERS

7he flavor of your cheese will determine the quality of these mouth-watering crackers. Choose the best cheddar you can get, and you'll be well rewarded. Serve the crackers as an appetizer or alongside a steaming bowl of soup.

½ cup (1 stick) unsalted butter, softened

2 cups (½ pound) grated extra-sharp cheddar cheese

1¼ cups unbleached flour

¼ teaspoon salt

⅛ teaspoon cayenne pepper

1 to 2 tablespoons water

Makes 4 dozen crackers

❶ In a large bowl, cream the butter with an electric mixer until soft and smooth. Beat in the cheese until blended.

❷ In a small bowl, mix together the flour, salt, and cayenne. Sprinkle into the butter mixture and beat just until combined. Pour in 1 to 2 tablespoons water, or just enough to help the dough cohere (it will be crumbly). Do not overbeat.

❸ Gather the dough into 2 balls, knead 2 or 3 times, then roll each ball into a cylinder 1½ inches in diameter. Wrap in wax paper or plastic wrap and chill the logs at least 30 minutes and up to 24 hours. Or wrap in plastic wrap and freeze for up to 2 weeks. If frozen, thaw the logs for 1 hour before using.

❹ Preheat the oven to 350°F. Slice the logs into rounds a little less than ¼ inch thick. Place on an ungreased baking sheet and bake 12 to 15 minutes, or until the edges are golden. Cool thoroughly on a wire rack. To store, place in a tin and keep at room temperature for up to 3 days. Or wrap in plastic and refrigerate for up to 2 weeks or freeze for up to 1 month.

TAMARI ALMONDS

*S*alty but not too salty,
and with an alluring overtone of spiciness. Great
for nibbling.

3 tablespoons tamari soy
sauce

1½ tablespoons vegetable oil

¼ teaspoon cayenne pepper

¾ teaspoon salt

4 cups (about 1¼ pounds)
whole, unblanched almonds

Makes 4 cups

❶ Combine the tamari, oil, cayenne, and salt in a large bowl. Stir in the almonds and coat well. Let sit 1 hour, stirring often.

❷ Preheat the oven to 300°F. With a slotted spoon, remove the almonds from the bowl and spread in a baking sheet in a single layer. Discard any remaining marinade. Bake 20 minutes, removing the baking sheet from the oven every 5 minutes or so and tossing the almonds with a spatula. (When done, the almonds will be somewhat dry and crusty looking and have a dark coating, but they should not be burnt.)

❸ Spoon the almonds into another baking sheet or onto a few plates, and let them cool completely. Store in an airtight container for up to 2 weeks, or wrap well and freeze up to 1 month.

SPICY MIXED NUTS

2 tablespoons unsalted butter

1 teaspoon chili powder

1 teaspoon ground cumin

½ teaspoon paprika

¼ teaspoon cayenne pepper

1 teaspoon salt

1 cup almonds

1 cup walnuts

1 cup raw or dry-roasted cashews *(see Note)*

1 cup pecans

Makes 4 cups

❶ Preheat the oven to 350°F.

❷ Melt the butter in a large skillet over medium heat. Add the spices and cook 30 seconds. Stir in the nuts and toss to coat well. Cook 2 minutes.

❸ Spread the nuts in one layer on a baking sheet. Bake 8 minutes. Remove from the oven and cool completely. Store in a tin or jar for up to 2 weeks, or freeze for up to 1 month.

☛*Note:* Raw cashews can be purchased in natural foods stores.

RUSSIAN-STYLE
MARINATED MUSHROOMS

My friend Sally Patterson, a Russian translator, introduced me to some memorable Russian dishes that she discovered while living in the Soviet Union. Here's one of my favorites: a tantalizing way of preparing mushrooms that doesn't involve any cooking. The mushrooms soak up the garlicky marinade and turn a rich, brown color. These make a popular hors d'oeuvre, served with toothpicks for nibbling, or a tasty first course, served on lettuce leaves.

½ cup olive oil

1 tablespoon red wine vinegar

3 garlic cloves, minced

⅓ cup minced fresh parsley

¼ teaspoon salt

Freshly ground black pepper to taste

1 pound very fresh mushrooms, rinsed and patted dry

Serves 4

❶ In a large bowl, whisk together the olive oil, vinegar, garlic, parsley, salt, and a liberal amount of pepper until blended.

❷ Cut any large mushrooms in half, and leave the others whole. Stir the mushrooms into the marinade and coat well. Cover and let sit at least 8 hours, but preferably for 24 hours. Stir periodically to coat with the marinade. (If marinating for a lengthy period, refrigerate after the first 8 hours.) Serve at room temperature.

EGGPLANT CAVIAR

*H*ere's another recipe
Sally Patterson brought back from the Soviet
Union. It's so delicious that my husband and I
inevitably eat the entire bowlful in one sitting.
Serve it Russian style with party-size pumper-
nickel bread or toasts.

¼ cup olive oil

1 medium onion, finely
diced

1 16-ounce can tomatoes,
finely chopped and well
drained

1 medium eggplant (about
1 pound), peeled and finely
diced

1 green bell pepper, finely
diced

2 tablespoons lemon juice

½ teaspoon salt

½ teaspoon sugar

Freshly ground black
pepper to taste

Serves 6 to 8

❶ Heat the oil in a large skillet over medium-high heat. Add the onion and sauté 5 minutes. Add the drained tomatoes and sauté 5 minutes more, stirring often.

❷ Lower the heat to medium, then stir in the remaining ingredients. Cover the pan and cook about 20 minutes, or until the eggplant is very tender. Stir periodically. Remove the cover of the pan and cook until all the juices have evaporated, another 5 minutes or so.

❸ Puree half the eggplant mixture in a blender or food processor and return to the pan. Stir very well to mix, then scrape into a serving bowl. Serve at room temperature.

MARINATED ROASTED PEPPERS

*S*poon these garlic-
soaked peppers on slices of French bread for a
divine appetizer — and be sure to fill the wine
glasses. If red bell peppers are not available or
are too expensive you can substitute additional
green peppers, although the mixture is more
striking if both colors are used.

1 pound (about 2 extra-
large) red bell peppers

1 pound (about 2 extra-
large) green bell peppers

⅓ cup olive oil

2 garlic cloves, pressed or
minced

½ teaspoon salt

Freshly ground black
pepper to taste

Makes 2 cups

❶ Place the peppers on a baking sheet and broil 1 to 3 inches from the flame or heating element until the peppers are blackened all over (this could take up to 20 minutes). You will have to turn the peppers every so often to char them evenly.

❷ When done, place the peppers in a paper or plastic bag and close it tight. Let the peppers sit 10 minutes; the steam they release will loosen the skins. Remove the peppers from the bag, then slip off the skins under cold running water. Pat the peppers very dry with paper towels.

❸ Core each pepper, then scrape out and discard the seeds. Cut the peppers into 1-inch squares and place in a bowl or jar.

❹ Add the remaining ingredients and toss to coat well. Marinate at least 2 hours before serving. These peppers can be refrigerated for up to 1 week, but be sure to bring them to room temperature before serving.

BLUE CHEESE LOG

8 ounces Neufchâtel or cream cheese, at room temperature

1 cup (about 4 ounces) crumbled blue cheese

2 tablespoons finely chopped walnuts

2 tablespoons minced fresh parsley

Serves 6 to 8

❶ Mash the cream cheese and blue cheese together with a fork until blended. Scrape the mixture onto a piece of wax paper and shape into a log 1½ inches in diameter. (The wax paper will help you roll the cheese into a cylinder. If the cheese mixture is too soft to handle, chill 20 minutes or so and shape again.)

❷ Combine the walnuts and the parsley in a small bowl. Sprinkle over the top and sides of the log. Slip the log onto a serving plate and serve at room temperature surrounded by crackers.

JALAPEÑO CHEESE NACHOS

These delicate crisps are made with flour tortillas instead of the corn variety, and this accounts for their unusual lightness. You can cook the tortillas up to three days in advance, but don't broil them with the cheese until you are ready to serve.

2 tablespoons vegetable oil

3 8-inch flour tortillas, cut into six wedges

1½ cups grated Monterey Jack cheese with jalapeño peppers

Serves 4

❶ With a pastry brush, lightly coat both sides of each tortilla wedge with oil. Place on cookie sheets and broil on both sides until lightly golden. (Do not let the tortillas get too brown.)

❷ When ready to serve the nachos, neatly sprinkle some of the grated cheese on each wedge. Broil just until melted. Serve immediately.

NACHOS WITH
SOUR CREAM

*P*lace this dish of nachos
in the center of the table and let everyone dip in.
So simple, yet downright addictive.

6 cups (about 4 ounces) corn
chips

1½ cups grated Monterey
Jack cheese

1 tablespoon minced fresh
cilantro (optional)

1 cup salsa

½ cup sour cream

Serves 4

❶ Preheat the oven to 400°F. Place the corn chips in one layer in a large shallow baking dish. Sprinkle on the cheese and cilantro. Bake 10 minutes, or until the cheese is melted.

❷ Remove from the oven, then drizzle the salsa all over the corn chips. Place little spoonfuls of sour cream all over the tops of the nachos, and serve immediately.

POTATO SKINS WITH
HORSERADISH DIP

*C*hildren love these
"fried potatoes," and they are much more nutritious than French fries or potato chips.

4 large baking potatoes,
scrubbed

. . . .

1 cup sour cream

1 tablespoon prepared
horseradish

Dash salt

Chili powder

. . . .

❶ Prick each potato in a few spots with a fork or knife and place in the oven. Set the oven at 400°F. (you don't have to preheat), and cook about 1 hour, or until tender.

❷ Meanwhile make the dip. Combine the sour cream, horseradish, and salt in a small bowl and mix to blend. Sprinkle on some chili powder, then chill the dip until ready to serve.

2½ tablespoons tamari soy sauce

¼ cup plus 2 tablespoons vegetable oil

Serves 4

❸ When the potatoes are done, remove them from the oven, then raise the temperature to 500°F. Let the potatoes cool until you can handle them. Cut each in half crosswise, then cut each half lengthwise into 4 pieces (each potato will yield 8 wedges). Slice some potato from each wedge, leaving about ¼ inch of potato on the skins. (Save the leftover potato flesh for potato pancakes. *See Note.*)

❹ Combine the tamari and oil in a small dish and, with a pastry brush, brush some of the mixture all over each potato wedge. Lay the wedges skin side down on a cookie sheet as you complete them. Liberally sprinkle chili powder on top of each wedge.

❺ Bake 15 to 20 minutes, or until crisp and golden brown. Serve on a platter surrounding the horseradish dip.

☞*Note:* To make potato pancakes, mix some melted butter, salt, and pepper into the potatoes and beat well with a fork. Form into patties and coat on both sides with flour. Fry over medium heat in a hot skillet that has been coated with some oil.

CHEESY POTATO SKINS
WITH SALSA DIP

*ere is another enticing
version of potato skins. These are extra crisp and
match well with a spicy salsa.*

4 baking potatoes

4 tablespoons unsalted
butter, melted

1 cup grated extra-sharp
cheddar cheese

Salsa

Serves 4

❶ Prick the potatoes, then bake them in a 400°F. oven until tender, about 1 hour. Remove from the oven and let cool a few minutes until easier to handle.

❷ Raise the oven temperature to 500°F. Slice the potatoes in half lengthwise, then in half again crosswise. Scoop out the potato flesh, leaving about ¼ inch on the skins. (Save the flesh for another use, such as potato pancakes. *See Note,* page 17.)

❸ Brush each potato shell—inside and out—with the melted butter, then place skin side down on a baking sheet. Bake 8 minutes, or until the wedges begin to brown.

❹ Remove the wedges from the oven, then place some grated cheese on each. Return to the oven and cook 5 minutes more, or until the cheese is bubbly. Serve warm with a bowl of salsa.

STUFFED MUSHROOMS

*S*herry and thyme accent
these juicy mushrooms. Be certain to cook them so
that they are tender throughout and have rendered
their juices.

12 large fresh mushrooms

3 tablespoons unsalted butter

2 garlic cloves, minced

1 small onion, minced

4 slices good-quality white bread

2 tablespoons minced fresh parsley

3 tablespoons dry sherry

½ teaspoon dried thyme

¼ teaspoon poultry seasoning

¼ teaspoon salt

Freshly ground black pepper to taste

Serves 3 to 4

❶ Preheat the oven to 350°F. Wipe the mushrooms clean with damp paper towels. Snap off the stems and mince them. Generously butter a pie plate or other shallow baking pan.

❷ Melt 2 tablespoons of the butter in a medium skillet over medium heat. Add the garlic and onion and sauté 10 minutes, stirring often. Add the minced mushroom stems and sauté 5 minutes more. Remove the pan from the heat.

❸ Toast the bread until golden. Let cool a few minutes, then tear it into tiny pieces and stir it into the onion mixture, pressing it to help it absorb the juices. Stir in the parsley, sherry, thyme, poultry seasoning, salt, and pepper.

❹ Place the mushroom caps in the prepared pie plate. Place a bit of the remaining tablespoon of butter inside each mushroom cap. Mound some stuffing in the caps, pressing it in firmly with your fingers.

❺ Bake 45 minutes, or until the mushrooms are brown, tender, and juicy.

STUFFED MUSHROOMS WITH SPINACH, FETA CHEESE, AND PINE NUTS

like to make these aromatic mushrooms bite size so they can be eaten easily with the fingers.

24 medium fresh mushrooms

1 10-ounce package frozen chopped spinach, thawed

⅓ cup crumbled feta cheese

1 tablespoon grated Parmesan cheese

3 tablespoons pine nuts

1½ tablespoons cold unsalted butter, cut into bits

Serves 4 to 6

❶ Preheat the oven to 375°F. Butter a shallow baking dish large enough to hold the mushrooms.

❷ Wipe the mushrooms clean with damp paper towels. Remove the stems and discard, or save for another use.

❸ With your hands, squeeze the spinach to remove all the moisture. When dry, place in a bowl, then stir in the feta and Parmesan cheeses. Set aside 24 of the pine nuts, then stir in the remainder.

❹ Stuff each mushroom with some of the spinach mixture. Press one pine nut into the top of each stuffed mushroom as a garnish. Press one bit of butter on top of each mushroom.

❺ Bake 30 minutes, or until brown and juicy. Serve warm.

CHEESE STRAWS

hese delicate puff pastry twists pair perfectly with wine or cocktails and are equally suitable as a snack for an informal occasion. They are easy to prepare and can be made up to one week in advance. Try standing them upright in a pretty glass tumbler.

1 sheet (about ½ pound) frozen store-bought puff pastry

¼ cup grated Parmesan cheese

¼ teaspoon dry mustard

A few pinches cayenne pepper

Makes 4 dozen cheese straws

❶ Thaw the puff pastry at room temperature until thoroughly defrosted but still cold, about 30 minutes. Carefully unroll it. Mix the Parmesan cheese, mustard, and cayenne together, then sprinkle half of it over the top of the pastry. With a rolling pin, lightly roll the cheese into the surface (the pastry will stretch a bit). Turn the pastry over and repeat.

❷ Preheat the oven to 350°F. Cut the dough in half (each half will now be about 5½ inches long). Using a ruler as a guide, cut the pastry into ⅓-inch-wide strips. (You should have about 48 5½ × ⅓-inch strips.)

❸ Twist each strip lengthwise to create a slight spiral, then place it on a baking sheet. Press the ends onto the sheet to help hold the spiral in place. Repeat with the remaining strips.

❹ Bake 15 minutes, or until puffed and golden brown. (The straws should not be dark brown, but they must be cooked through.) Transfer to a rack and cool to room temperature. The straws can be stored in an airtight tin for up to 1 week, or refrigerated or frozen for a few weeks.

CHOPPED BLACK OLIVE SPREAD
(OLIVADA)

This dark, lusty spread makes a wonderful appetizer spooned on toasted French bread slices and served with a heady red wine. In this version I use two types of olives because I have found that the bland-tasting canned olives pair beautifully with the pungent oil-cured variety.

*Try spreading a thin layer of **Olivada** on sandwich bread or a hard roll. Top with sliced tomato and Swiss cheese for a superlative sandwich.*

4 ounces (about 1 cup) oil-cured black olives *(see Note)*

1 6-ounce can pitted black olives

2½ tablespoons olive oil

1 to 2 garlic cloves, pressed

Pinch each dried oregano, basil, rosemary, and thyme

Freshly ground black pepper to taste

Makes about 1 cup

❶ Pit the oil-cured olives one at a time by placing each on a cutting board and resting the flat side of a large knife on it. Thump the knife with the heel of your hand—the olive will split and the pit can be removed easily. When done, you should have a generous ½ cup of pulp.

❷ Drain the canned olives in a strainer and shake out all the liquid.

❸ Combine the olive oil and garlic in a blender or processor and process until smooth and creamy or cloudy in appearance.

❹ Add the olives and herbs and blend just until the mixture reaches a nice spreading consistency. The *Olivada* should not be perfectly smooth. (Turn off the machine and scrape down the sides as necessary if you're using a blender.) Scrape the paste into a serving bowl and season with black pepper. Let sit 20 minutes before serving, or cover and chill for up to 1 week. Bring to room temperature before using.

☛*Note:* If oil-cured olives are unavailable, you can substitute a more assertive brine-cured variety such as Greek Kalamata olives.

MOLDED WHITE BEAN PÂTÉ

*P**retty enough for enter-
taining and quick enough for a last-minute appetizer, this pâté has a wonderful blend of Mediterranean flavors.*

2 15-ounce cans cannellini
(white kidney) beans, rinsed
and thoroughly drained

2 garlic cloves, pressed or
minced

2 tablespoons olive oil

¾ teaspoon dried thyme

¼ teaspoon good-quality
Hungarian paprika

½ teaspoon tamari soy sauce

Freshly ground black
pepper to taste

2 tablespoons grated
Parmesan cheese

2 tablespoons minced fresh
parsley

Toasted French bread slices,
or other toast

Serves 4 to 6

❶ Place the drained cannellini beans in a medium
bowl and thoroughly mash them with a fork.

❷ Sauté the garlic in the olive oil just until lightly
golden, about 30 seconds. Do not let it brown. Mix
the garlic into the beans, along with all the other
ingredients *except* 1 tablespoon parsley and the
bread.

❸ Line a 1½-cup mold or bowl with wax paper.
Scrape the pâté into it and press it down with the
flat side of a knife. Cover with wax paper and chill at
least 30 minutes. Unmold onto a plate and sprinkle
on the remaining tablespoon of parsley, pressing it
lightly into the pâté. Surround the pâté with the
toast. (I like to let the pâté sit at room temperature
for a while so that it's served cool, not cold.)

GREEN GODDESS DIP

This pretty, pale-green dip has a cottage cheese base, making it a low-calorie alternative to the traditional mayonnaise-laden version. When pureed in a blender or food processor, cottage cheese assumes a perfectly smooth texture that makes it ideal for dips. Serve this in an attractive bowl and surround it with a bright assortment of crudités such as carrots, celery, red peppers, and cauliflower.

1 cup cottage cheese

¼ cup milk

1 tablespoon fresh lemon juice

1 tablespoon mayonnaise

¼ cup thinly sliced scallions (mostly green parts)

¼ cup finely chopped fresh parsley

Salt

Freshly ground black pepper

Fresh parsley sprig, for garnish

Makes 1⅓ cups

❶ Put the cottage cheese, milk, lemon juice, mayonnaise, scallions, and parsley in the container of a blender or food processor and blend until perfectly smooth. If you are using a blender, you will have to turn if off frequently and scrape down the sides.

❷ Scrape the dip into a serving bowl and season to taste with salt and pepper. Cover and chill at least 1 hour before serving, to allow the flavors to meld. Just before serving, stir the dip to smooth out the consistency. If the dip is too thick, stir in a few drops of milk. Serve garnished with the parsley sprig. The dip will keep 3 days in the refrigerator.

CREAMY CURRY DIP

A pale-yellow dip with a smooth cottage cheese base, this mildly spicy version looks pretty served in a contrasting bowl surrounded by colorful crudités.

1 cup cottage cheese

¼ cup milk

¼ cup sour cream

1 garlic clove, minced

½ teaspoon minced fresh ginger

1 teaspoon turmeric

¼ teaspoon ground cumin

¼ teaspoon ground coriander

½ teaspoon sugar

Makes 1½ cups

❶ Combine all of the ingredients in a blender or food processor and blend until perfectly smooth. Turn off the machine and scrape down the sides as necessary.

❷ Scrape the dip into a serving bowl. Cover and chill for 30 minutes before serving to allow the flavors to blend. This dip will keep, refrigerated, for up to 3 days.

SPICY PEANUT DIP

Peanuts have a natural affinity with spices, as many Asian and African cuisines attest. Try this feisty dip with a colorful assortment of raw vegetables surrounding it.

1 cup crunchy natural-style peanut butter

¾ cup water

2 tablespoons fresh lemon juice

1 teaspoon soy sauce

3 garlic cloves, minced

2 teaspoons minced fresh ginger

Dash cayenne pepper

Fresh parsley or cilantro sprig, for garnish

Makes 2 cups

❶ Combine all of the ingredients except the herb sprig in a large bowl and stir with a fork until blended. If the mixture is too thick, add ¼ cup water, or enough to create a good dipping consistency.

❷ Scrape the dip into a serving bowl, cover, and let sit at room temperature at least 30 minutes before serving. If you must chill the dip, bring it to room temperature before serving. (If it becomes very thick, thin it with a little more water.) Garnish with the parsley or coriander sprig. The peanut dip will keep in the refrigerator for 3 days.

☛*Variations:* Leftover Spicy Peanut Dip is delicious served with steamed or sautéed mixed vegetables (or sliced, raw salad vegetables such as cucumber, crunchy lettuce, green pepper, onion, and tomato). Stuff them into pita bread halves, then pour the dip over them.

BEAN AND SALSA DIP

You can control the spiciness of this dip by using mild, medium, or hot salsa (I prefer hot). Hot pita triangles are my favorite accompaniment, but corn chips or your favorite crackers will also be delicious with this robust dip.

2 cups freshly cooked kidney beans (page 161), or 1 16-ounce can kidney beans, rinsed and drained

2 tablespoons olive oil

2 to 3 tablespoons water

4 tablespoons salsa

1 teaspoon chili powder

¼ teaspoon ground cumin

Fresh parsley or cilantro sprigs, for garnish

Hot pita triangles

Makes 1½ cups

❶ Combine the beans, oil, and 2 tablespoons of the water in a blender or food processor and blend until almost smooth. (You will have to turn off the machine and scrape down the sides a few times.) Add the remaining tablespoon water if necessary, but be careful not to thin the mixture too much; it should be somewhat like thick mashed potatoes.

❷ Scrape the mixture into a serving bowl and stir in 3 tablespoons of the salsa, the chili powder, and the cumin until well mixed. Spoon the remaining tablespoon salsa on top of the dip, and gently swirl it into the surface to make a decorative look. Cover and chill at least 1 hour to develop the flavors. Just before serving, garnish with the parsley or coriander sprigs. Serve on a platter and surround with hot pita triangles.

SOUPS

o my mind, a savory pot of homemade soup is a creation worthy of center stage. I often serve generous bowlfuls as a main course, accompanied by soup's natural mates: salad and bread. The soup, salad, and bread trio makes a wonderfully complete meal, both nutritionally and aesthetically (see Soup Meals, page 236).

For the busy cook, soup can be a godsend. All the recipes in this chapter can be doubled easily, and the extra portion can be refrigerated and served within a week. Freezing a batch of soup is another smart approach, one that you'll be thankful for when a hectic day comes along and you have no time at all to cook. The following soups freeze well: Curried Zucchini Soup (page 33), Mexican Vegetable Stew (page 35), Split Pea Soup (page 38), and Lentil Soup with Garlic (page 40). Undercook them slightly, cool completely before freezing for up to one month, and adjust the seasoning after thawing and reheating.

MUSHROOM SOUP WITH HERBS

This light version of mushroom soup is a luscious change from the more common cream of mushroom soup.

3 tablespoons unsalted butter

2 medium onions, finely chopped

2 garlic cloves, minced

1 pound (about 6 cups) thinly sliced fresh mushrooms

1 carrot, minced

1 celery rib, very thinly sliced

3 tablespoons unbleached flour

7 cups vegetable stock *(see Note)*

½ teaspoon salt

Freshly ground black pepper to taste

¾ cup heavy cream

2 tablespoons minced fresh chives

½ teaspoon minced fresh thyme, or ¼ teaspoon dried thyme

Dash cayenne pepper

3 tablespoons sherry

Serves 4 as a main course

❶ Melt the butter in a large stockpot over medium heat. Add the onions and garlic and sauté 10 minutes, or until very tender. Stir often.

❷ Raise the heat to medium-high. Stir in the mushrooms, carrot, and celery and cook until the mushrooms are tender and juicy, about 10 minutes.

❸ Sprinkle on the flour and stir to mix. Cook 2 minutes, stirring frequently. Stir in the vegetable stock, salt, and pepper and bring the soup to a boil, scraping the bottom of the pot with your spoon to remove any flour bits that have stuck. Cook 30 minutes at a lively simmer, stirring often. Remove 2 cups soup from the pot and puree in a blender or food processor, then return to the pot.

❹ Mix in the cream, chives, thyme, cayenne, and sherry. Bring to a boil again, then remove from the heat. Serve immediately, or reheat when ready to serve.

☛*Note:* Vegetable stock can be made with powdered vegetable stock base, available at health food stores.

CURRIED ZUCCHINI SOUP

The base of this spicy soup has an almost satinlike consistency, with chunks of zucchini throughout. Its apparent richness belies the fact that it's very low in calories.

3 tablespoons vegetable oil

2 large onions, diced

2 garlic cloves, minced

1 teaspoon minced fresh ginger

1 teaspoon turmeric

1 teaspoon ground cumin

1 teaspoon ground coriander

Few dashes cayenne pepper

5 cups vegetable stock *(see Note, page 32)*

5 medium zucchini (about 2 pounds), quartered lengthwise and finely diced

½ teaspoon salt

Plain yogurt, for garnish

Serves 4 as a main course

❶ Heat the oil in a large stockpot over medium heat. Add the onions, garlic, and ginger and sauté 10 minutes, stirring often. Sprinkle on the turmeric, cumin, coriander, and cayenne and cook 2 minutes.

❷ Pour in the stock and bring to a boil. Add the zucchini and salt and cook, partially covered, 30 minutes, or until the zucchini is very tender. Remove the cover and let the soup cool 10 minutes.

❸ Puree half the soup in a blender or food processor, then return it to the pot. Reheat until hot, then serve in bowls with a generous spoonful of yogurt on each serving.

CURRY. The word kari in Tamil means sauce, but in the West we use the word curry as a catchall term to describe Indian food prepared with a mixture of spices. Many Westerners erroneously think curry powder is a spice in itself. Rather, it is a blend of between three and twenty spices, including turmeric, coriander seed, cumin seed, cayenne pepper, mustard seed, cardamom, ginger, black pepper, fennel seed, fenugreek, cloves, and cinnamon. Curry powder is not used in India; it is an item packaged for Western cooks. Indian cooks artfully combine many of the above spices in varying proportions to season each dish. On rare occasions I use curry powder to accent a simple dip or cream soup, but most often I toast a mélange of spices in oil or butter to achieve the multidimensional character for which Indian dishes are renowned.

The amount of cayenne pepper in a recipe determines how hot your curry will be. The heat can be adjusted easily to suit your taste. Start off with 1/8 teaspoon cayenne pepper, taste the finished dish, then sprinkle on more if needed.

MEXICAN VEGETABLE STEW

This fragrant stew, unlike most vegetable soups and stews, doesn't demand much chopping and so can be prepared quickly and easily. Like most soups, it tastes even better when served the next day, so don't hesitate to make it in advance. I like to sprinkle cheddar cheese and broken corn chips on top.

¼ cup olive oil

4 garlic cloves, minced

2 large onions, diced

1 teaspoon ground cumin

1 28-ounce can imported plum tomatoes (about 3 cups), roughly chopped, with their juice

8 cups vegetable stock (*see Note,* page 32)

½ teaspoon salt

Freshly ground black pepper to taste

2 carrots, thinly sliced

3 medium zucchini, cut lengthwise into sixths, then into 1-inch chunks

2 cups freshly cooked kidney beans (page 161), or 1 15-ounce can kidney beans, rinsed and drained

2 cups fresh or frozen corn kernels

Grated cheddar cheese (optional)

Corn chips (optional)

Serves 4 as a main course

❶ In a 6- to 8-quart pot, heat the olive oil over medium heat. Sauté the garlic, onions, and cumin 10 minutes, stirring often.

❷ Add the tomatoes with their juice, the vegetable stock, salt, and pepper and bring to a boil.

❸ Add the carrots and cook 15 minutes, then add the zucchini and cook 5 to 10 minutes, or until the zucchini is tender, not mushy.

❹ Add the kidney beans and corn and cook 2 minutes. Remove 2 cups of the stew, puree it in the blender or food processor, then return it to the pot. This will nicely thicken the stew. Taste to adjust the seasoning. If desired, sprinkle on grated cheese and break a few corn chips over each serving.

CHILLED AVOCADO SOUP

*Here is a creamy,
delicious soup for avocado lovers. It is the quickest soup I know of — particularly wonderful on a hot summer day because it doesn't require any cooking.*

1 medium ripe Haas avocado (black pebble-skinned variety)

2 cups buttermilk

2 tablespoons lemon juice

½ teaspoon salt

Few dashes cayenne pepper

1 medium tomato, seeded and finely diced

1 small scallion, very thinly sliced

Serves 4 as a first course

❶ Cut the avocado in half lengthwise and discard the pit. Insert the handle of a teaspoon between the flesh and the skin and move it around until the flesh is released from the skin.

❷ Combine the avocado flesh, buttermilk, lemon juice, salt, and cayenne in a blender or food processor and puree until smooth. Pour into a medium bowl.

❸ Set aside about a tablespoon each of the tomato and scallion. Stir the remaining tomato and scallion into the soup. Cover the bowl and chill at least 1 hour before serving.

❹ Serve with some of the reserved tomato and scallions topping each serving.

CURRIED BARLEY AND MUSHROOM SOUP

I f you prefer this soup only slightly spicy, reduce the amount of cayenne to a few dashes.

3 tablespoons vegetable oil

2 medium onions, diced

2 garlic cloves, minced

2 teaspoons minced fresh ginger

12 ounces (about 4½ cups) chopped mushrooms

2 teaspoons ground coriander

1½ teaspoons ground cumin

1 teaspoon turmeric

½ teaspoon ground cardamom

⅛ teaspoon cayenne pepper

1 bay leaf

Freshly ground black pepper to taste

1 cup uncooked barley

8 cups water

1 teaspoon salt

1 tablespoon tamari soy sauce

1 tablespoon unsalted butter

2 egg yolks

½ cup milk

Minced fresh chives, scallions, parsley, or cilantro

Serves 4 as a main course

❶ Heat the oil in a large stockpot over medium heat. Sauté the onions, garlic, and ginger 3 minutes. Add the mushrooms and sauté 5 minutes.

❷ Sprinkle in the spices and the bay leaf and mix well. Cook 1 minute, stirring often. Add the barley and cook another 2 minutes, stirring all the while. Add the water, salt, and tamari, then cover the pot. Cook the soup at a lively simmer 1 hour, or until the barley is tender. Discard the bay leaf.

❸ Remove the pot from the heat, then swirl in the butter. Mix the egg yolks with the milk, then slowly stir the mixture into the soup *(see Note)*. Serve immediately, garnished with your choice of herbs.

☛ *Note:* If you want to prepare this soup in advance, add the yolk mixture just before serving. The soup can be reheated once it has been thickened with the yolks, but it must not boil.

SPLIT PEA SOUP

*Cumin lends a delicious
nuance to this delectable soup. However, you can
omit it and still have a full-flavored soup.*

2 cups (1 pound) green split
peas

10 cups water

2 bay leaves

3 tablespoons olive oil

3 medium onions, finely
diced

3 garlic cloves, minced

2 teaspoons ground cumin

2 celery ribs, finely diced

3 carrots, finely diced

2 tablespoons tamari soy
sauce

Freshly ground black
pepper to taste

Salt

2 tablespoons unsalted
butter

Serves 4 as a main course

❶ In a large stockpot, combine the split peas, water, bay leaves, and 1 tablespoon of the olive oil. Cover the pot, bring to a boil (watch for overflowing foam), then reduce the heat to a lively simmer. Cook 1 hour, stirring occasionally.

❷ Meanwhile, heat the remaining 2 tablespoons olive oil in a medium skillet. Add the onions and garlic and sauté 10 minutes, or until tender. Stir in the cumin and cook, stirring frequently, 2 additional minutes.

❸ After the peas have cooked 1 hour, stir in the onion mixture and all of the remaining ingredients except the butter. Cook, uncovered, an additional 30 to 35 minutes, or until the soup has a somewhat smooth consistency and the vegetables are tender. Be aware that the soup will thicken in each serving bowl as it cools, so don't let it get too thick. Remove the bay leaves. Just before serving, taste for salt, then stir in the butter.

SPINACH SOUP WITH SEMOLINA CHEESE DUMPLINGS

The most widely available semolina is packaged farina, easily found in supermarkets.

DUMPLINGS

1 cup milk

2 tablespoons unsalted butter

½ cup semolina (farina)

3 tablespoons grated Parmesan cheese

¼ teaspoon freshly grated nutmeg

½ teaspoon salt

1 egg, beaten

SOUP

3 tablespoons olive oil

2 medium onions, finely diced

10 cups vegetable stock (*see Note,* page 32)

1 pound loose fresh spinach (stems removed), finely chopped, *or* 1 10-ounce package frozen chopped spinach, thawed and squeezed dry

1 teaspoon salt

Freshly ground black pepper to taste

1 tablespoon unsalted butter

Grated Parmesan cheese

Serves 4 as a main course

❶ To make the dumplings: In a medium saucepan bring the milk and butter to a boil. Lower the heat to simmer, then slowly sprinkle in the semolina, stirring all the while with a wire whisk. Whisk in the Parmesan cheese, nutmeg, and salt and cook just until the mixture begins to clump, about 2 minutes. Remove from the heat and whisk in the egg. Scrape the mixture into a medium bowl, cover, and chill at least 2 hours or overnight.

❷ To make the soup: Heat the olive oil in a large stockpot and sauté the onions until very tender, about 10 minutes. Add the stock and bring to a boil.

❸ Meanwhile, form the dumplings into compact ½-inch balls by squeezing some of the chilled dough between your hands, then rolling it between your palms. You should have about 20 dumplings. Set aside on a platter.

❹ Add the chopped spinach to the boiling stock. When the soup returns to a boil, drop in the dumplings. Cover the pot and cook 15 minutes. Remove the cover and stir in the salt, pepper, and butter. Serve with Parmesan cheese sprinkled over each bowl.

LENTIL SOUP WITH GARLIC

This is my sister-in-law Beth's memorable version of lentil soup. Its deep, lingering flavor soothes the soul.

¼ cup olive oil

4 garlic cloves, minced

3 large onions, diced

7½ cups water

1 cup lentils, picked over and rinsed

4 carrots, thinly sliced

3 celery ribs, thinly sliced

¼ cup tomato paste mixed with ½ cup water

1 tablespoon tamari soy sauce

½ teaspoon salt

Freshly ground black pepper to taste

2 tablespoons unsalted butter

Serves 4 as a main course

❶ Heat the olive oil in a large stockpot over medium heat. Add the garlic and onions and sauté 10 minutes, or until the onions are very soft and begin to brown. Stir often.

❷ Add all of the remaining ingredients except the butter. Raise the heat and bring the soup to a boil, stirring often. Reduce the heat to simmer and cook 45 minutes, or until the carrots are very tender and the soup has thickened.

❸ Just before serving, add the butter and stir until melted.

BILLIE'S FRESH PEA SOUP

My friend Billie Cherni-coff, a highly inventive cook, created this soup. The use of sweet peas rather than dried, split peas lends this soup a special flavor. Mint and lemon also give it a refreshing spring accent, although it can be made during any season.

3 tablespoons olive oil

2 medium onions, diced

2 garlic cloves, minced

5 cups vegetable stock *(see Note, page 32)*

1 large potato, peeled and diced

6 cups (3 10-ounce packages) frozen peas

⅛ teaspoon cayenne pepper

½ teaspoon salt

Juice of ½ lemon

½ cup heavy cream

1 teaspoon minced fresh dill

1 tablespoon minced fresh mint

Additional fresh dill or mint, for garnish

Serves 4 as a main course

❶ Combine the olive oil, onions, and garlic in a large stockpot and sauté over medium heat until the onions begin to get tender, about 10 minutes.

❷ Pour in the vegetable stock, add the potatoes, then bring to a boil. Reduce the heat to simmer and cook until the potatoes are tender, about 20 minutes.

❸ Stir in the peas, cayenne, and salt and cook 5 minutes more. Remove 1 cup of the soup and set aside. Let the rest of the soup cool a bit, then puree in batches until perfectly smooth. Return the pureed soup to the pot, then stir in the reserved cup of soup, lemon juice, cream, dill, and mint. Reheat until piping hot but not boiling. Serve garnished with mint or dill.

CORN CHOWDER

Scallions greatly enhance the flavor of this thick soup, so be certain to include them. Making the soup a few hours in advance will allow the flavors to meld.

1 tablespoon unsalted butter

2 tablespoons olive oil

2 medium onions, finely diced

2 garlic cloves, minced

1 teaspoon good-quality sweet paprika

4 cups vegetable stock *(see Note,* page 32)

2 large potatoes, peeled and finely diced (about 2½ cups)

1 celery rib, very thinly sliced

1 bay leaf

½ teaspoon salt

1 teaspoon sugar

Freshly ground black pepper to taste

4 cups frozen corn kernels

5 scallions, very thinly sliced

1 cup milk

¼ teaspoon dried thyme

Few dashes cayenne pepper

¼ cup sour cream

Serves 4 as a main course

❶ In a large stockpot, combine the butter, olive oil, onions, and garlic and sauté over medium heat until the onions are tender but not brown, about 10 minutes. Sprinkle on the paprika, toss, and cook 1 minute.

❷ Add the stock, potatoes, celery, bay leaf, salt, sugar, and pepper. Cook, partially covered, until the potatoes are tender, about 15 minutes. Stir in the corn and scallions, and cook 2 minutes more. Remove the bay leaf.

❸ Scoop out 2 cups of the chowder and set it aside. Puree the remainder and return it to the pot. Stir in the reserved chowder, the milk, thyme, and cayenne pepper. Cook 5 minutes more. Serve in bowls with a spoonful of sour cream on top.

BREADS, MUFFINS, ETC.

No matter how delicious the bread at the corner bakery, there is nothing quite so satisfying as a loaf of homemade bread or a batch of warm, fragrant muffins fresh from the oven. The kitchen abounds with inviting aromas, conveying a delightful feeling of comfort.

For the cook who is pressed for time, bread baking can be quick and simple if quick leavenings such as baking powder and baking soda are used instead of yeast. Quick breads don't always have to be sweet, although the popular zucchini, pumpkin, or banana breads are great served for breakfast, snacks, or teatime. Savory breads such as Herb Oat Bread (page 48), Jalapeño Cheddar Soda Bread (page 54), Irish Brown Bread (page 53), and Rich Cream Cheese Biscuits (page 59) make wonderful accompaniments to steaming bowls of homemade soup and fresh, colorful salads.

When I'm busy but want to make bread, scones, or muffins, I approach the recipe in stages.

First I prepare the pan, at some other time I combine the dry ingredients, and later on I mix together the wet ingredients. When I'm ready to bake, I preheat the oven. About twenty minutes later I combine the wet and dry ingredients, then pop the batter into the oven. When approached in this way, bread baking is a breeze.

WHOLE WHEAT MOLASSES BREAD

Spread softened butter on this ultraquick, nutritious bread and serve it for breakfast or tea, or alongside soup for supper. This is also a good choice for parents seeking a wholesome snack for their kids.

2 cups whole wheat flour

1½ teaspoons baking powder

½ teaspoon baking soda

1½ teaspoons caraway seeds (optional)

¾ teaspoon salt

1 large egg

1 cup buttermilk, or plain low-fat yogurt

½ cup molasses

¼ cup vegetable oil

Makes one 9×5-inch loaf

❶ Preheat the oven to 350°F., then butter a 9×5-inch (1½-quart) loaf pan.

❷ In a large bowl, thoroughly combine the flour, baking powder, baking soda, caraway seeds, and salt.

❸ In a medium bowl, beat the egg, then beat in the buttermilk or yogurt, molasses, and oil. Scrape this into the flour mixture and stir just until combined.

❹ Pour the batter into the prepared loaf pan and bake 40 minutes, or until a knife inserted in the center of the loaf comes out dry. Cool on a rack 10 minutes, then remove the loaf from the pan and cool at least 1 hour before slicing.

HERB OAT BREAD

1¼ cups rolled oats

1 cup unbleached flour

¼ cup whole wheat flour

2 teaspoons baking powder

½ teaspoon baking soda

¾ teaspoon salt

½ teaspoon dried basil

½ teaspoon dried oregano

½ teaspoon dried dill

⅛ teaspoon crumbled dried rosemary

¼ cup vegetable oil

¼ cup honey

1¼ cups plain low-fat yogurt

2 large eggs, beaten

Makes one 9×5-inch loaf

❶ Preheat the oven to 375°F. Butter and flour a 9×5-inch (1½-quart) loaf pan.

❷ Place the oats in a blender or food processor and grind until almost powdery. Pour into a large bowl and mix in the flours, baking powder, baking soda, salt, and herbs.

❸ In a small saucepan, combine the oil and the honey and heat just until blended. Remove from the heat and stir in the yogurt and beaten eggs.

❹ Pour into the flour mixture and stir just until evenly moistened. Do not overbeat. Scrape into the prepared pan.

❺ Bake 40 minutes, or until a knife inserted in the center of the bread comes out clean. (If the top of the bread begins to darken before it finishes cooking, lay a sheet of foil over the top of the pan and bake until done.) Cool on a wire rack 10 minutes before removing from the pan. Cool completely before slicing.

☛*Variations:* A great gift idea is to bake this bread 25 minutes in 3 5×3×2-inch baby loaf pans (disposable aluminum ones work well). Cool thoroughly when done, and wrap individually. To make Sage Onion Bread, substitute ¼ teaspoon powdered sage and ¼ cup fresh minced onion instead of the basil, dill, and rosemary.

MUFFIN AND QUICK-BREAD TIPS

☞ Preheat your oven for at least fifteen minutes to be certain it is hot enough. A hot oven ensures high rising.

☞ Generously butter your loaf pan. Butter the insides *and* the top of your muffin pan.

☞ Mix dry ingredients thoroughly, then mix wet ingredients thoroughly. Combine just until evenly moistened. Don't overbeat.

☞ You can't make muffin or quick-bread batter ahead of time because once the leavening (baking powder or baking soda) begins to work—which is almost instantly upon the addition of a liquid—the batter must be baked immediately. But you can do a few steps in advance: butter the pan; mix all of the dry ingredients in one bowl and the wet ingredients in another, keeping them separate. Just be certain not to let the leavening come in contact with the wet ingredients until you are ready to bake.

☞ Although bread, muffins, scones, and biscuits always taste best when fresh, they can be frozen with good results. After they have cooled completely, wrap them in aluminum foil, then place in a plastic bag. Freeze for up to one month. Defrost at room temperature.

ZUCCHINI BRAN BREAD

A moist and not-too-sweet version of zucchini bread with added bran. Freeze one of the loaves for a future treat.

3 large eggs

1½ cups sugar

1 tablespoon vanilla extract

1 cup vegetable oil

4 cups (about 2 large) grated zucchini

2 cups unbleached flour

½ cup whole wheat flour

½ cup bran

1 teaspoon baking powder

1 teaspoon baking soda

1 teaspoon salt

2 teaspoons cinnamon

1 cup finely chopped walnuts

Makes two 9×5-inch loaves

❶ Preheat the oven to 350°F. Butter and flour 2 9×5-inch (1½-quart) loaf pans.

❷ In a large bowl, beat the eggs and sugar until light and fluffy. Beat in the vanilla and the oil, then stir in the zucchini.

❸ In a medium bowl, thoroughly combine the remaining ingredients. Stir into the zucchini mixture just until evenly moistened. Scrape into the prepared pans. Bake 50 minutes, or until a knife inserted in the center of a loaf comes out clean. Let sit 5 minutes before turning out onto a wire rack. Cool completely before slicing.

OATMEAL RAISIN BREAD

This moist and buttery bread is excellent spread with cream cheese and served either open faced or made into bite-size sandwiches.

1½ cups rolled oats

1 cup unbleached flour

2 teaspoons baking powder

½ teaspoon baking soda

1 teaspoon cinnamon

¾ teaspoon salt

1 cup raisins

¼ cup vegetable oil

⅓ cup honey

1¼ cups buttermilk, or plain low-fat yogurt

2 large eggs, beaten

Makes one 9×5-inch loaf

❶ Preheat the oven to 375°F. Butter and flour a 9 × 5-inch (1½-quart) loaf pan.

❷ Grind the oats in a blender or food processor until almost powdery. Pour into a large bowl and thoroughly mix in the flour, baking powder, baking soda, cinnamon, and salt. Stir in the raisins.

❸ Combine the oil and honey in a small saucepan and heat until just blended. Stir in the buttermilk or yogurt and the beaten eggs, then pour into the flour mixture and stir until just blended. Do not overmix. Scrape into the prepared pan.

❹ Bake 45 to 50 minutes, or until a knife inserted in the center comes out clean. (If the bread begins to get too brown before it has finished cooking, lay a sheet of foil over the top of the pan and continue baking.) Cool on a wire rack 10 minutes, then slide a knife around the periphery of the bread and slip it out of the pan. Cool at least 1½ hours before slicing.

APPLE BREAD

*A*lmond extract gives this bread a wonderful accent without overpowering the fresh taste of the apples.

1½ cups unbleached flour

½ cup whole wheat flour

1 teaspoon baking powder

1 teaspoon baking soda

½ teaspoon salt

2 large eggs

½ cup vegetable oil

⅔ cup firmly packed light brown sugar

½ cup orange juice

¾ teaspoon almond extract

⅔ cup raisins

2 cups finely chopped peeled apple (about 3 apples)

Makes one 9 × 5-inch loaf

❶ Preheat the oven to 350°F. Butter and flour a 9 × 5-inch (1½-quart) loaf pan. In a medium bowl, thoroughly combine the flours, baking powder, baking soda, and salt.

❷ Beat the eggs in a large bowl, then beat in the oil, brown sugar, orange juice, and almond extract.

❸ Stir in the flour mixture, then mix in the raisins and apples until evenly coated. Scrape into the prepared pan. Bake 70 minutes, or until a knife inserted in the center of the loaf comes out clean. (If the bread begins to get dark on top before it has finished cooking, place a sheet of foil over it and continue baking.) Let cool on a rack 10 minutes before removing from the pan. Cool completely before slicing, about 2 hours.

IRISH BROWN BREAD

In Ireland, brown bread is made with a unique whole meal flour that is unmatched in this country for both its flavor and texture. I have discovered that a combination of oats, wheat germ, and whole wheat flour produces an almost identical loaf that is as hauntingly good.

1¼ cups unbleached flour, plus additional for sprinkling

1 cup whole wheat flour

½ cup rolled oats

¼ cup toasted wheat germ

1½ teaspoons baking soda

¾ teaspoon salt

4 tablespoons cold unsalted butter

1⅓ cups buttermilk, or plain low-fat yogurt

Makes one 7-inch round loaf

❶ Preheat the oven to 425°F. Lightly dust a baking sheet with flour and set it aside.

❷ In a large bowl, very thoroughly mix together the flours, oats, wheat germ, baking soda, and salt.

❸ Cut the butter into bits, then rub it into the flour mixture with your fingertips until it is evenly incorporated.

❹ Stir in the buttermilk or yogurt until blended, then turn the dough onto a lightly floured surface and knead for 1 minute. Sprinkle on more flour as necessary to prevent sticking, but let the dough remain soft.

❺ Roll the dough into a ball, then flatten into a 7-inch circle. Sprinkle some unbleached flour on top of the circle, then lightly spread it around with your hand. With a sharp knife cut a shallow X on top. Bake 30 minutes, then cool on a wire rack at least 2 hours before slicing.

JALAPEÑO CHEDDAR SODA BREAD

A delicate, buttery texture and hint of spiciness make this bread absolutely delicious.

2¼ cups unbleached flour

¼ cup whole wheat flour

1 teaspoon baking soda

1 teaspoon baking powder

¾ teaspoon salt

4 tablespoons cold unsalted butter, cut into bits

2 cups grated extra-sharp cheddar cheese

4 fresh or canned jalapeño peppers, seeded and minced *(see Note)*

1 large egg, beaten

1¼ cups buttermilk, *or* plain low-fat yogurt

Makes one 7-inch round loaf

❶ Preheat the oven to 400°F. Rub a little flour into an 8-inch circle on a baking pan and set aside.

❷ In a large bowl, thoroughly combine the flours, baking soda, baking powder, and salt. Drop in the butter bits, and rub them into the flour mixture with your fingertips until coarse crumbs are formed.

❸ Stir in the cheese and jalapeño peppers until evenly distributed. Combine the egg with the yogurt and stir it into the mixture until just evenly moistened.

❹ Scrape the dough onto a lightly floured surface and knead for 1 minute, or until the dough is just smooth and pliable. Pat it into a 7-inch circle, then place on the floured baking sheet. Cut a shallow **X** in the top.

❺ Bake 35 minutes, or until golden brown. For best results, let cool about 1 hour and serve warm.

☛*Note:* Wear rubber gloves when handling hot peppers so that the volatile oils don't get on your fingers and later come into contact with your eyes. Jalapeños burn!

IRISH GOLDEN RAISIN BREAD

olden raisins impart a special flavor to this raisin-filled version of Irish soda bread.

2 cups unbleached flour, plus extra for sprinkling

¼ cup bran or toasted wheat germ

1 teaspoon baking soda

½ teaspoon salt

4 tablespoons cold unsalted butter

1 cup golden raisins

1 cup buttermilk, *or* plain low-fat yogurt

Makes one 6-inch round loaf

❶ Preheat the oven to 400°F. Lightly sprinkle some flour on a baking sheet and rub it into an 8-inch circle.

❷ In a large bowl, mix together the flour, bran or wheat germ, baking soda, and salt. Cut the butter into bits, letting it drop into the flour. Stir in the butter to coat it, then rub it into the flour mixture with your fingertips until it is the consistency of coarse meal.

❸ Toss in the raisins and thoroughly coat them with flour. Stir in the buttermilk or yogurt and mix until incorporated. Turn the dough onto a lightly floured surface and knead for a full 1 minute, sprinkling on more flour as necessary to prevent sticking.

❹ Shape the dough into a ball, then flatten it into a 6-inch circle. Place on the floured baking sheet and sprinkle on a teaspoon or so of flour, spreading it evenly over the top. Cut a shallow X on top of the dough. Bake 35 minutes, or until the bread is a rich golden brown.

❺ Wrap the bread in a cotton kitchen towel (this softens the crust) and let cool 1 hour. Unwrap the loaf and continue to cool on a wire rack. This bread is best if allowed to sit for a few hours before slicing.

APPLESAUCE OATMEAL BREAD

*O**atmeal is the source of
this bread's intriguing nubby texture.***

1½ cups rolled oats

1¼ cups unbleached flour

1 teaspoon baking powder

¾ teaspoon baking soda

½ teaspoon cinnamon

½ teaspoon freshly grated nutmeg

⅔ teaspoon salt

⅔ cup raisins

2 large eggs

½ cup firmly packed light brown sugar

¼ cup vegetable oil

1 cup applesauce

Makes one 9×5-inch loaf

❶ Preheat the oven to 350°F. Butter and flour a 9×5-inch (1½-quart) loaf pan.

❷ In a large bowl, thoroughly combine the oats, flour, baking powder, baking soda, cinnamon, nutmeg, salt, and raisins.

❸ In a medium bowl, beat the eggs. Beat in the brown sugar, oil, and applesauce. Pour this into the oat mixture and stir until just evenly moistened. Scrape into the prepared loaf pan.

❹ Bake 50 minutes, or until a knife inserted in the center of the loaf comes out dry. Let sit 5 minutes, then remove from the pan and cool completely on a wire rack, at least 2 hours.

PUMPKIN BREAD WITH STREUSEL TOPPING

Freeze one of these loaves for a ready-made breakfast or snack.

½ cup vegetable oil

¾ cup sugar

¾ cup firmly packed light brown sugar

3 large eggs

1 teaspoon vanilla extract

1 15- to 16-ounce can solid-packed pumpkin

2½ cups unbleached flour

1½ teaspoons baking powder

1½ teaspoons baking soda

¾ teaspoon salt

1½ teaspoons cinnamon

½ teaspoon freshly grated nutmeg

1 cup finely chopped walnuts or pecans

⅔ cup raisins

STREUSEL TOPPING

⅓ cup unbleached flour

⅓ cup sugar

4 tablespoons cold unsalted butter, cut into bits

Makes two 9×5-inch loaves

❶ Preheat the oven to 350°F. Butter and flour two 9×5-inch (1½-quart) loaf pans.

❷ In a large bowl, beat together the oil, sugars, eggs, and vanilla using an electric mixer. Beat in the pumpkin until thoroughly blended. Beat in the remaining bread ingredients until evenly moistened. Scrape into the prepared pans.

❸ To make the topping: Combine the flour and sugar in a small bowl. With your fingers, rub the butter into the flour mixture until coarse crumbs are formed. Sprinkle the crumbs on top of each loaf. Bake 50 to 55 minutes, or until a knife inserted in the center of a loaf comes out clean. Cool on a wire rack 10 minutes before removing from the pans. Cool thoroughly before slicing.

BANANA DATE BREAD

A favorite in our house, this dark, gutsy banana bread filled with dates and walnuts is delicious plain or slathered with cream cheese.

1 cup whole wheat flour

1 cup unbleached flour

1 teaspoon baking soda

½ teaspoon baking powder

¼ teaspoon salt

½ teaspoon cinnamon

¼ teaspoon ground cloves

¼ teaspoon freshly grated nutmeg

1 cup chopped pitted dates

1 cup finely chopped walnuts

½ cup vegetable oil

½ cup honey

2 large eggs

1 cup mashed banana (about 3 small bananas)

1 teaspoon vanilla extract

Makes one 9×5-inch loaf

❶ Preheat the oven to 350°F. Butter and flour a 9×5-inch (1½-quart) loaf pan.

❷ In a large bowl thoroughly combine the flours, baking soda, baking powder, salt, cinnamon, cloves, and nutmeg. Stir in the dates and walnuts.

❸ In a medium bowl, beat the oil and honey together until smooth. Beat in the eggs, banana, and vanilla until well mixed. Pour into the flour mixture and stir just until evenly moistened. Scrape the batter into the prepared loaf pan.

❹ Bake 60 to 70 minutes, or until a knife inserted in the center of the loaf comes out clean. (If the loaf begins to get too dark before it has finished cooking, lay a sheet of aluminum foil over the top and continue baking.) Let stand on a wire rack 10 minutes before removing from the pan. Cool completely before slicing, about 2 hours.

RICH CREAM CHEESE BISCUITS

Buttery, flaky, and unforgettable — everything you could want in a biscuit.

1¾ cups unbleached flour

¼ cup whole wheat flour

1 tablespoon baking powder

½ teaspoon salt

4 tablespoons cold unsalted butter

2 tablespoons cold cream cheese

1 large egg, beaten

¾ cup milk

Makes 12 biscuits

❶ In a large bowl combine the flours, baking powder, and salt and mix very well. Cut the butter and cream cheese into bits and mix into the flour mixture to coat. With a pastry cutter or your fingers, rub the bits into the flour until coarse crumbs are formed.

❷ Stir in the beaten egg with a fork, then slowly pour in the milk, stirring all the while. Let the dough sit for 1 minute to absorb the liquid.

❸ Turn the dough onto a slightly floured surface and knead 5 or 6 times to make it pliable.

❹ Pat the dough into a round or oblong shape ½ to ¾ inch thick (measure it). With a 2½-inch biscuit cutter or cup, cut out the biscuits and place them, with edges touching, on an ungreased cookie sheet. You should have about 12 biscuits.

❺ Preheat the oven to 375°F. Place the cookie sheet in the freezer for 10 minutes, or in the refrigerator for at least 15 minutes and up to 4 hours before baking. (Cold biscuits in a hot oven ensure flakiness.) Bake 20 to 25 minutes, or until lightly golden. Serve immediately.

CHEESE SCONES

*C**heese inside and out accounts for the sharp flavor of these Scottish "biscuits."***

1¾ cups unbleached flour

¼ cup whole wheat flour

2 teaspoons baking powder

1 teaspoon dry mustard

¼ teaspoon salt

Dash cayenne pepper

3 tablespoons cold unsalted butter

1 cup grated extra-sharp cheddar cheese

1 large egg, beaten

½ cup milk, plus extra for brushing

Makes 8 large scones

❶ Preheat the oven to 400°F. Lightly butter a baking sheet.

❷ In a large bowl, thoroughly combine the flours, baking powder, mustard, salt, and cayenne. Cut the butter into bits and rub it into the mixture until it resembles coarse crumbs.

❸ Stir in all but 2 tablespoons of the grated cheese. Mix the egg with the milk and stir in until just evenly moistened.

❹ Turn the dough onto a lightly floured surface, and knead a few times, or just until pliable. Pat into a ½-inch-thick circle and cut the circle into 8 triangles. Place the scones on the baking sheet. Brush the tops lightly with some milk, then sprinkle on the reserved cheese.

❺ Bake 17 minutes, or until golden brown. Serve warm, not hot.

ORANGE CURRANT SCONES

These scones are incredibly delicate and flavorful. Try them with a steamy pot of Earl Grey tea.

1¾ cups unbleached flour

¼ cup whole wheat flour

2 tablespoons sugar

1½ teaspoons baking powder

½ teaspoon baking soda

¼ teaspoon salt

4 tablespoons cold unsalted butter

½ cup currants

1 large egg

Grated rind of 1 orange

⅔ cup buttermilk, *or* plain low-fat yogurt

Milk for brushing on tops

Makes 10 scones

❶ Preheat the oven to 400°F. Lightly butter a baking sheet.

❷ In a large bowl, combine the flours, sugar, baking powder, baking soda, and salt. Cut the butter into bits and with your fingertips work it into the mixture until it resembles coarse meal. Stir in the currants.

❸ Beat the eggs with the orange rind. Beat in the buttermilk or yogurt. Stir this into the flour mixture just until evenly moistened.

❹ Turn the dough onto a lightly floured surface and knead a few seconds. Pat it into a circle ¾ inch thick. With a 2½-inch biscuit cutter, form the scones. Place them on the prepared baking sheet and lightly brush the tops with some milk.

❺ Bake 15 minutes, or until the scones are a rich golden brown. Serve warm.

APPLESAUCE WHEAT GERM MUFFINS

These are big, fat, impressive muffins, exceptionally moist and light.

1½ cups unbleached flour

1 cup toasted wheat germ

2 teaspoons baking powder

½ teaspoon baking soda

¾ teaspoon salt

1 teaspoon cinnamon

¼ teaspoon freshly grated nutmeg

½ cup raisins

1 large egg

½ cup firmly packed light brown sugar

⅓ cup vegetable oil

1 cup applesauce

½ cup milk

TOPPING

2 teaspoons sugar

¼ teaspoon cinnamon

Makes 12 muffins

❶ Preheat the oven to 425°F. Generously butter the insides and top of a regular-size (⅓-cup) muffin pan.

❷ In a large bowl, thoroughly combine the flour, wheat germ, baking powder, baking soda, salt, cinnamon, nutmeg, and raisins.

❸ In a medium bowl, beat the egg, then beat in the brown sugar, oil, applesauce, and milk. Mix with the dry ingredients just until evenly moistened. Spoon the batter into the muffin cups.

❹ For the topping, combine the sugar and cinnamon, and sprinkle on top of each muffin.

❺ Bake 17 minutes, or until a knife inserted in the center of a muffin comes out clean. Let sit a few minutes before removing from pan. Serve warm, not hot.

CHEDDAR CORN MUFFINS

These are light and moist, with a mild but irresistible cheese accent. They are equally good served for breakfast or with chili. If you want a more traditional corn muffin, just leave out the cheese.

1 cup unbleached flour

1 cup yellow cornmeal

1 tablespoon baking powder

½ teaspoon salt

¼ cup sugar

1 large egg

1 cup milk

4 tablespoons unsalted butter, melted

1¼ cups grated extra-sharp cheddar cheese

Makes 12 muffins

❶ Preheat the oven to 425°F. Butter the insides and the top of a regular-size (⅓-cup) muffin pan.

❷ In a large bowl, thoroughly combine the flour, cornmeal, baking powder, salt, and sugar.

❸ In a medium bowl, beat the egg. Beat in the milk, and the melted butter. Combine with the dry ingredients until just evenly moistened. Do not overmix. Stir in 1 cup of the cheese.

❹ Immediately spoon the batter into the muffin cups. Evenly sprinkle the remaining ¼ cup of cheese on top of the muffins.

❺ Bake 17 minutes, or until a knife inserted in the center of a muffin comes out clean. Serve hot or warm.

CARROT BRAN MUFFINS

These bran muffins are grainy but light and have just the right amount of molasses to make their flavor deep but not overbearing. Grated carrots add flavor and texture.

1½ cups bran

1½ cups whole wheat pastry flour, or ¾ cup whole wheat flour plus ¾ cup unbleached white flour

2 teaspoons baking powder

¼ teaspoon cinnamon

½ teaspoon salt

⅔ cup raisins

2 medium carrots, grated

1 large egg

⅓ cup vegetable oil

½ cup unsulphured molasses

⅓ cup honey

¾ cup milk

Makes 12 muffins

❶ Preheat the oven to 400°F. Generously butter the insides and top of a regular-size (⅓-cup) muffin pan.

❷ In a large bowl, combine the bran, flour, baking powder, cinnamon, and salt and mix very well. Stir in the raisins and carrots to coat evenly.

❸ Beat the egg in a medium bowl, then beat in the oil, molasses, honey, and milk. Combine with the dry ingredients until just evenly moistened. Do not overstir.

❹ Spoon the batter into the prepared muffin pan and bake 17 minutes, or until a knife inserted in the center of a muffin comes out clean. Cool 5 minutes before removing from pan.

OATMEAL MUFFINS

he irresistible brown sugar–oatmeal flavor of these muffins is heightened by the crunchy topping. A favorite with children.

1¼ cups rolled oats

1¼ cups buttermilk, *or* plain low-fat yogurt

1 cup unbleached flour

1½ teaspoons baking powder

½ teaspoon baking soda

½ teaspoon cinnamon

½ teaspoon salt

½ cup raisins

1 large egg

½ cup firmly packed light brown sugar

5 tablespoons unsalted butter, melted

TOPPING

1 tablespoon unsalted butter, melted

1 tablespoon firmly packed light brown sugar

¼ cup rolled oats

⅛ teaspoon cinnamon

Makes 12 muffins

❶ Preheat the oven to 400°F. In a large bowl, beat together the oats and buttermilk or yogurt, and let sit 15 minutes. Meanwhile, butter the insides and top of a regular-size (⅓-cup) muffin pan.

❷ In a small bowl, thoroughly combine the flour, baking powder, baking soda, cinnamon, salt, and raisins.

❸ Beat the egg, brown sugar, and melted butter into the oat mixture. Stir in the dry ingredients until just evenly combined. Spoon the batter into the muffin pan.

❹ Combine the ingredients for the topping and sprinkle some on top of each muffin. Bake 17 minutes, or until a knife inserted in the center of a muffin comes out clean. Let sit 5 minutes before removing from the pan. Serve warm, not hot.

SPICY PUMPKIN MUFFINS

Remember these moist, flavorful muffins at Halloween. Top them with cream cheese icing for a great kids' treat.

1½ cups unbleached flour

½ cup whole wheat flour

1 tablespoon baking powder

½ teaspoon salt

2 teaspoons cinnamon

½ teaspoon ground ginger

½ teaspoon freshly grated nutmeg

¼ teaspoon ground cloves

1 large egg

½ cup firmly packed light brown sugar

1 cup fresh or canned pumpkin puree *(see Note)*

½ cup vegetable oil

½ cup milk

¾ cup raisins

½ cup finely chopped walnuts

Makes 12 muffins

❶ Preheat the oven to 400°F. Butter the insides and top of a regular-size (⅓-cup) muffin pan.

❷ In a large bowl, thoroughly combine the first 8 ingredients.

❸ In a medium bowl, beat the egg. Beat in the brown sugar, then stir in the pumpkin, oil, and milk until well mixed.

❹ Mix the pumpkin mixture into the dry ingredients until just combined. Don't overmix. Stir in the raisins and all but 2 tablespoons of the walnuts.

❺ Spoon the batter into the muffin cups, then sprinkle the remaining walnuts on top of the muffins. Bake 15 to 17 minutes, or until a knife inserted in the center of a muffin comes out clean. Let sit 2 minutes before removing from pan. Serve warm or at room temperature, not hot.

☞*Note:* Leftover pumpkin puree can be frozen in 1-cup portions for future use.

FRUIT JUICE MUFFINS

Only frozen apple juice concentrate, grated apple, and raisins sweeten these light, fruity muffins.

1½ cups unbleached flour

½ cup whole wheat flour

2 teaspoons baking powder

½ teaspoon baking soda

½ teaspoon salt

½ teaspoon cinnamon

½ cup raisins

½ cup finely chopped walnuts

1 medium apple, peeled and grated

1 large egg

⅓ cup vegetable oil

½ cup frozen apple juice concentrate

½ cup water

Makes 12 muffins

❶ Preheat the oven to 425°F. Butter the insides and top of a regular-size (⅓-cup) muffin pan.

❷ In a large bowl, thoroughly combine the flours, baking powder, baking soda, salt, and cinnamon. Stir in the raisins, walnuts, and grated apple.

❸ In a medium bowl, beat the egg, then beat in the oil, apple juice concentrate, and water. Stir this into the dry mixture until just evenly moistened. Spoon the batter into the muffin pan.

❹ Bake 15 minutes, or until a knife inserted in the center of a muffin comes out clean. Cool for a few minutes before removing from the pan. Serve warm, not hot.

SUBSTANTIAL SALADS AND SALAD DRESSINGS

A favorite quick meal in our house that allows advance preparation is a hearty grain or pasta salad. These one-dish meals need little to accompany them because they are composed of so many satisfying ingredients. An appetizer beforehand and some delicious bread served alongside the salad is enough to complete the meal.

Although I serve these substantial salads year round, I particularly enjoy them during the warm-weather months when I can appreciate the minimal amount of cooking they require. Sometimes I cook the pasta or grain the night before or in the early morning, to keep my kitchen cool throughout the day. Then I finish the salad making later on. (If you cook pasta in advance, be certain to coat it with a little oil after draining, to prevent sticking.)

Spread on a bed of sprightly greens such as red- or green-leaf lettuce or lightly dressed bite-size spinach leaves, these salads make attractive buffet or potluck supper dishes. They are also an appealing way to introduce less adventurous eaters to unfamiliar grains such as bulghur, kasha, and couscous.

The salad dressings in this chapter are intended for mixed green salads. Creamy dressings mate well with crisp, sturdy greens such as romaine and iceberg lettuces and fresh spinach, while vinaigrette-style dressings work well with the aforementioned greens, and also with lighter-textured lettuces such as Boston, green-leaf, and red-leaf varieties.

You can pour oil-and-vinegar-based dressings on the entire salad, toss, and serve immediately. Creamy dressings should be served at the table in a sauceboat so that each person can pour on the amount he or she desires.

WILD RICE SALAD WITH APPLES AND WALNUTS

*This crunchy, nutty salad
is surprisingly light and has a tantalizing flavor.
Serve it on a bed of curly green-leaf lettuce.*

1 cup wild rice

2 cups water

1 tablespoon vegetable oil

¼ teaspoon salt

1 cup coarsely chopped walnuts

1 celery rib, sliced

4 scallions, thinly sliced

1 cup raisins

1 medium red apple (not Delicious), cored and diced

Grated rind of 1 lemon

. . . .

3 tablespoons fresh lemon juice

2 garlic cloves, pressed

½ teaspoon salt

Freshly ground black pepper to taste

⅓ cup olive oil

. . . .

Green-leaf lettuce (optional)

Serves 4 as a main course

❶ Put the wild rice in a strainer and rinse under cold water. Place it in a medium saucepan along with the water, oil, and salt. Cover, bring to a boil, and reduce the heat to simmer. Cook 50 minutes, or until the rice is tender and all the water has been absorbed. (When wild rice is done, it has a tender yet nubby texture.)

❷ Meanwhile, combine the walnuts, celery, scallions, raisins, apple, and lemon rind in a large bowl. In a jar with a tight-fitting lid, combine the lemon juice, garlic, salt, pepper, and olive oil and shake vigorously. Pour half of this dressing on the apple mixture and toss well.

❸ When the rice is done, let it cool until just warm. Combine with the fruit mixture and pour on the remaining dressing. Let sit at least 1 hour before serving at room temperature, on a bed of lettuce if desired.

COUSCOUS AND VEGETABLE SALAD WITH ORANGE AND GARLIC

he mingling of flavors and colors in this salad is hypnotic. The orange, garlic, and basil are an unforgettable combination. Paired with the raisins and toasted almonds, these ingredients result in a triumphant blending of flavors that will gratify the most discerning palate. On a sultry summer day, what better than a memorable dish that requires barely any cooking?

1½ cups couscous

½ cup raisins

1 teaspoon turmeric

2 cups boiling water

⅔ cup sliced almonds

2 cups chick-peas (page 161), *or* 1 15-ounce can chick-peas, rinsed and drained

3 scallions, thinly sliced

2 medium tomatoes, halved, seeded and diced

. . . .

⅓ cup fresh lemon juice

⅓ cup olive oil

2 garlic cloves, minced

Grated rind of 1 orange

1 tablespoon minced fresh basil, *or* 2 teaspoons dried

½ teaspoon salt

Freshly ground black pepper to taste

Green-leaf lettuce

Serves 4 as a main course

❶ Place the couscous, raisins, and turmeric in a large bowl, then pour the boiling water over them and stir well. Cover with foil or a large plate and let sit 5 minutes. Fluff with a fork, cover again, and let sit 10 minutes longer.

❷ Stir in the almonds, chick-peas, scallions, and tomatoes.

❸ Combine the lemon juice, olive oil, garlic, orange rind, basil, salt, and pepper and beat to blend. Pour over the couscous mixture and toss. Cover and chill at least 30 minutes, or up to 24 hours, before serving. Serve mounded on leaves of green-leaf lettuce.

COUSCOUS. Couscous (pronounced koos'-koos) is a grain product made by mixing semolina (coarse flour made from hard durum wheat) and water to form tiny granules. To add to the confusion, couscous is also the name of a traditional North African dish composed of couscous, vegetables, and meat.

Very popular in North African cooking, couscous has an appealing, delicate texture and buttery flavor. It is delicious when made into a salad, pilaf, or main course mixed with vegetables.

If you want to include a grain in your meal planning and have finicky eaters to feed, couscous's palatability makes it a good choice.

COLD SZECHUAN NOODLES WITH SHREDDED VEGETABLES

*M*arinated Chinese noo-
dle dishes have such a delicious flavor and texture
that few people can resist their appeal. This is an
excellent main course for a hot day because the
noodles can be cooked early in the morning (or
the night before) when it is cool and left to marinate until serving time.

This is the kind of dish that begs for improvisation. Try different vegetables — whatever is fresh-
est at the market.

1 pound noodles such as
spaghetti, linguine, or
fresh Chinese noodles, if
available (vermicelli and
capellini are too fine)

4 tablespoons tamari soy
sauce

4 tablespoons oriental
sesame oil

1 tablespoon Chinese rice
vinegar *or* other vinegar

1 tablespoon sugar

½ teaspoon chili oil

1 red bell pepper, cored and
shredded

3 scallions, thinly sliced

2 carrots, grated

1 scallion branch, for
garnish *(see Note)*

Serves 4 as a main course

❶ In a (6- to 8-quart) stockpot, bring several quarts
of water to a boil and cook the noodles until al
dente — that is, tender yet slightly firm to the bite.
Do not overcook. (If you are using fresh Chinese
noodles, you need to cook them only for a few
minutes.)

❷ Mix together 3 tablespoons of the tamari, 3 tablespoons of the sesame oil, and the vinegar, sugar,
and chili oil in a cup. When the noodles are done,
drain them thoroughly in a colander, shaking out as
much water as you can. Drop them into a large
bowl, pour on the sauce, and toss the noodles carefully with tongs to coat them well. Marinate at least
2 hours, or up to 24 hours, before serving, tossing
occasionally. Cover and chill the noodles if they are
prepared more than 4 hours in advance.

❸ If the noodles have been chilled, bring them to
room temperature before serving. Mix the remaining 1 tablespoon soy sauce and 1 tablespoon sesame
oil together and pour over the noodles. Stir in the
red peppers, two-thirds of the sliced scallions, and
half the grated carrots.

ORIENTAL SESAME OIL. Do not confuse this strong-tasting oil with mild, cold-pressed sesame oil that is usually sold in natural foods stores. Oriental sesame oil, dark brown in color, is made from roasted sesame seeds and has a distinct toasted sesame aroma. Just a few teaspoons will enliven the flavors of any Chinese dish. Unlike light-colored sesame oil, oriental sesame oil will keep indefinitely and need not be refrigerated.

❹ To serve, mound the noodles on a serving platter and sprinkle on the remaining scallions and carrots. Place the scallion branch on top.

☛*Note:* To make a scallion branch, trim the top from a scallion so that the remaining white-and-pale-green piece is about 3 inches long. Cut off the root section. Insert the tip of a small, sharp knife about ¼ inch from the center of the scallion and slice upward. Repeat 3 or 4 times to create thin strips. Turn the branch and repeat with the other end. The point is to leave about ½ inch in the center intact and shred the ends. Drop the branch into ice water for about 30 minutes so the ends will curl. Remove the branch and shake out any water before placing it on the noodles.

CRUNCHY LENTIL SALAD

K eeping the lentils slightly crunchy and dressing them with a small amount of olive oil, lemon juice, and spices contributes to this salad's light consistency. I often serve this alongside a baked potato for a quick, complete meal.

1 cup lentils, picked over and rinsed

5 cups water

1 bay leaf

1 celery rib, finely diced

1 carrot, minced

¼ cup finely diced red onion

2 tablespoons minced fresh parsley

¼ cup fruity olive oil

2 tablespoons fresh lemon juice

1 garlic clove, pressed or minced

¼ teaspoon dried thyme

¼ teaspoon ground cumin

Salt to taste

Freshly ground black pepper to taste

Serves 4 as a main course

❶ In a medium saucepan, combine the lentils, water, and bay leaf. Bring to a boil and cook, uncovered, 15 minutes, or until the lentils are tender but still crunchy. Stir occasionally. Pour into a colander and discard the bay leaf. Drain the lentils very well, and let them sit 5 minutes or so to be certain all the water has drained out.

❷ Place the lentils in a serving bowl and gently stir in the celery, carrot, onion, and parsley.

❸ Mix together the olive oil, lemon juice, garlic, thyme, cumin, salt, and pepper. Pour onto the lentil mixture, and carefully toss. Serve at room temperature.

PENNE AND BROCCOLI SALAD WITH CREAMY GARLIC DRESSING

*The Parmesan cheese
and creamy dressing that coat this salad
are a welcome change from the more common
vinaigrette that usually dresses pasta salads.*

1 bunch broccoli, cut into small flowerets and stalks peeled and diced (about 5 cups)

½ pound (3 cups) *penne* (quill-shaped pasta)

1 medium tomato, seeded and cubed

⅓ cup pine nuts

1 tablespoon minced fresh basil, or 1 teaspoon dry

⅔ cup Creamy Garlic Dressing (page 93)

2 tablespoons grated Parmesan cheese

Salt to taste

Freshly ground black pepper to taste

Serves 4 as a main course

❶ Bring a large stockpot of water to a boil. Drop in the broccoli and blanch until tender but still crunchy, about 2 minutes. Remove with a slotted spoon and place in a bowl. Rinse under cold running water until chilled. Drain thoroughly, then pat dry with paper towels. Place in a large serving bowl.

❷ Cook the *penne* in the boiling water until al dente. Drain in a colander, then chill under cold water. Drain again, then pat with paper towels to absorb moisture. Place in the bowl with the broccoli.

❸ Stir in the tomato, pine nuts, and basil. Mix the dressing with the Parmesan cheese and pour on the salad. Season with salt and pepper. Let sit at least 30 minutes before serving. If you are going to wait longer, cover and chill until 30 minutes before serving, then bring to room temperature.

BULGHUR SALAD WITH CORN, ZUCCHINI, AND SHREDDED BASIL

I prefer to use dark, coarse-grain American bulghur for this salad because its color is more appealing and harmonious with corn than that of the lighter-colored Middle Eastern variety.

The inimitable flavor of fresh basil stands tall in this dish and mates wonderfully with the corn, zucchini, and tomatoes.

1½ cups coarse-grain bulghur

1½ cups frozen corn kernels, thawed

1 tomato, cut into small cubes

1 cup very thinly sliced zucchini rounds, cut into sixths

3 tablespoons finely shredded fresh basil

¼ cup thinly slivered red onion

⅓ cup olive oil

¼ cup lemon juice

2 garlic cloves, pressed

½ teaspoon salt

Freshly ground black pepper to taste

Lettuce leaves, for garnish

Serves 4 as a main course

❶ Place the bulghur in a large bowl. Pour boiling water over it to cover by 2 inches. Let soak 30 minutes, or until tender. Remove all of the soaking liquid by placing the bulghur, in batches, in cheesecloth or a cotton towel and squeezing it dry. Or place it in a strainer and press out the liquid with the back of a large spoon. Place the strained bulghur in a large serving bowl.

❷ Stir in the corn, tomato, zucchini, basil, and onion. In a separate bowl, beat together the olive oil, lemon juice, garlic, salt, and pepper. Pour it over the salad and mix well. Let sit 30 minutes, or cover and chill for up to 24 hours, then bring to room temperature before serving. Place lettuce leaves on individual plates and spoon the salad on top.

BASIL ICE CUBES. Have too much fresh basil and don't want to stuff any more pesto into your freezer? Try pureeing fresh basil leaves with a little water in your blender or food processor, then pouring the mixture into an ice cube tray. Freeze until solid, then pop out the cubes and store them in a plastic bag in the freezer. Basil ice cubes can be dropped into soups or sauces to imbue them with that fresh basil flavor.

MEDITERRANEAN PASTA SALAD WITH CHICK-PEAS AND ROASTED PEPPERS

Roasted peppers, chick-peas, olives, tomatoes, and herbs fill this salad in which the pasta serves only as a backdrop. A good crusty bread would add the right touch.

½ pound *rotini* (short corkscrew pasta)

1 large green bell pepper

1 large red bell pepper

1 19-ounce can chick-peas, rinsed and well drained

1 medium tomato, diced

16 oil-cured black olives

2 tablespoons minced fresh parsley

½ cup slivered red onion

DRESSING

⅓ cup olive oil

2 tablespoons red wine vinegar

1 teaspoon Dijon mustard

3 garlic cloves, pressed

½ teaspoon dried oregano

¼ teaspoon crushed red pepper flakes

½ teaspoon salt

Freshly ground black pepper to taste

Serves 4 to 6 as a main course

❶ Roast, peel, seed, and chop the peppers as described through step 3 on page 14.

❷ Meanwhile, cook the *rotini* until al dente in a large stockpot of boiling water. Drain the pasta in a colander and shake vigorously to remove all the water. Place in a large bowl. Stir in the peppers, chick-peas, tomato, olives, parsley, and onion.

❸ In a jar with a tight-fitting lid, combine all the ingredients for the dressing. Shake vigorously, then pour over the pasta mixture and toss well. Serve the salad warm or at room temperature.

BROCCOLI AND RICE SALAD

Raisins are a surprise ingredient in a number of savory Italian dishes. In this light salad they add a welcome sweetness in counterpoint to the broccoli and garlic. Remember this salad when you have leftover cooked rice.

½ cup long-grain brown rice

1½ cups water

1 teaspoon vegetable oil

¼ teaspoon salt

1 bunch broccoli (flowerets cut into small pieces and stems discarded) (about 3½ cups)

⅓ cup raisins

1 carrot, minced

⅓ cup slivered red onion

2 tablespoons minced fresh basil, *or* 1 teaspoon dried

DRESSING

2 garlic cloves, pressed

2 tablespoons red wine vinegar

1 teaspoon Dijon mustard

⅓ cup olive oil

¼ teaspoon salt

Freshly ground black pepper to taste

Serves 2 to 3 as a main course

❶ In a small saucepan, combine the rice, water, oil, and salt. Cover the pan, bring to a boil, and reduce the heat to a low simmer. Cook undisturbed until all of the water is absorbed, about 45 minutes. Spoon the rice into a large serving bowl and let cool to warm; refrigerate until cold.

❷ Steam the broccoli flowerets until tender yet still bright green. Immediately immerse them in cold water to stop further cooking. Drain and pat dry with a cotton or paper towel. Stir into the rice along with the raisins, carrot, onion, and basil.

❸ Combine the ingredients for the dressing in a jar with a tight-fitting lid. Shake vigorously, then pour over the salad. Toss to coat. Let the salad marinate 30 minutes or so before serving. Serve at room temperature.

TORTELLINI SALAD PRIMAVERA

*L et your imagination
and the season's bounty determine your vegetable
selection; just be sure not to overcook any of the
vegetables, and strive for contrasting colors.*

8 asparagus stalks, peeled
and cut into 1-inch lengths

1 carrot, thinly sliced

1 cup small broccoli
flowerets

1 cup sliced yellow squash

1 medium tomato, seeded
and cubed

½ cup frozen peas, thawed

1 celery rib, thinly sliced

2 scallions, thinly sliced

⅓ cup pine nuts

2 tablespoons minced dill

1 pound fresh or frozen
cheese tortellini

DRESSING

2 garlic cloves, pressed

3 tablespoons fresh lemon
juice

1 tablespoon red wine
vinegar

½ cup olive oil

¼ teaspoon sugar

½ teaspoon salt

Freshly ground black
pepper to taste

Lettuce leaves (optional)

Serves 4 as a main course

❶ Bring a large stockpot of water to a boil. Drop in the asparagus, carrot, and broccoli and let sit 1 minute. Remove with a slotted spoon and drop into a bowl of ice water. Drain and dry on paper towels.

❷ Drop the yellow squash into the boiling water for 30 seconds, then remove, cool, and dry as above. Place the blanched vegetables in a serving bowl large enough to hold the tortellini also. Mix in the tomato, peas, celery, scallions, pine nuts, and dill.

❸ Drop the tortellini into the boiling water and cook until just al dente, not mushy, about 5 minutes for fresh tortellini and 15 minutes for frozen. Drain in a colander, then run cold water over the tortellini. Drain again very well. Stir the tortellini into the vegetables.

❹ To make the dressing, combine all of the dressing ingredients in a jar with a screw-on top. Shake very well. The dressing can be made up to 8 hours before using. Pour over the tortellini and vegetables and coat thoroughly. Chill until ready to serve. For a pretty presentation, serve on a bed of curly lettuce leaves.

MARINATED KASHA AND VEGETABLE SALAD

A light, attractive salad in which the nutty flavor of kasha marries perfectly with lemon and thyme. Try this on a hot day when you crave something fresh and flavorful that requires minimal cooking.

3 cups vegetable stock *(see Note), or* water

½ teaspoon salt

1½ cups medium-granulation kasha

½ cup plus 1 tablespoon olive oil

12 ounces (about 4½ cups) mushrooms, quartered

Grated rind of 1 lemon

3 tablespoons fresh lemon juice

1 garlic clove, minced

1 teaspoon dried thyme

Freshly ground black pepper to taste

½ cup minced fresh parsley

1 celery rib, thinly sliced

2 carrots, minced

3 scallions, very thinly sliced

⅔ cup finely chopped walnuts

1 cup frozen peas, thawed

Lettuce leaves (optional)

Serves 4 to 6 as a main course

❶ Bring the vegetable stock or water to a boil in a medium pot. Pour in the salt and the kasha, cover the pot, and reduce the heat to a simmer. Cook until all of the water is absorbed, about 10 minutes. Spoon the kasha into a large bowl and let it cool. Stir it occasionally to break up any lumps that might form.

❷ Heat 1 tablespoon of the olive oil in a large skillet over medium-high heat. Add the mushrooms and sauté until the juices rendered evaporate and the mushrooms begin to stick to the pan. Spoon the mushrooms into a bowl and stir in the remaining ½ cup olive oil, lemon rind, lemon juice, garlic, thyme, and pepper.

❸ Mix the parsley, celery, carrots, scallions, walnuts, and peas into the kasha. Pour in the mushrooms and their marinade and toss thoroughly. Cover and chill 30 minutes, or up to 24 hours, before serving. Serve at room temperature on lettuce leaves, if desired.

☞*Note:* Vegetable stock can be made with powdered vegetable stock base, available at health food stores.

CAPONATA

Try serving this cold Sicilian eggplant salad on lettuce leaves as a salad course, or surrounded by French bread pieces for a robust appetizer. And remember it for your next picnic.

¼ cup plus 2 tablespoons olive oil

1 medium (1¼-pound) eggplant, peeled and cut into ½-inch cubes

2 celery ribs, thinly sliced

2 large onions, finely diced

2 tablespoons capers

½ cup (about 8 large) chopped green olives

2 tablespoons tomato paste

½ cup water

¼ cup red wine vinegar, *or* balsamic vinegar

2 teaspoons sugar

Serves 6 to 8 as an appetizer and 4 as a main course

❶ Heat ¼ cup of the olive oil in a large skillet over medium-high heat. Add the eggplant and cook, tossing often, until tender, about 10 minutes. (The eggplant will absorb the oil and begin to stick, but don't add any more oil, just keep tossing.) When done, the eggplant will be cooked through but not mushy. Scoop it out of the pan and onto a platter. Reduce the heat to medium.

❷ Pour the remaining 2 tablespoons olive oil into the skillet and stir in the celery and onions. Sauté until tender, about 10 minutes, scraping up any crusty bits of eggplant that may have stuck to the pan.

❸ Return the eggplant to the skillet, then toss in the capers and olives. In a small bowl, combine the tomato paste, water, vinegar, and sugar and stir into the eggplant mixture. Simmer 10 minutes, stirring occasionally. Scrape the eggplant mixture into a large bowl, and chill at least 2 hours. Bring to room temperature before serving. Caponata can be kept refrigerated for up to 3 days.

TORTELLINI SALAD WITH PESTO

*S*erve this salad, always
popular at cookouts and informal parties, in a
pretty bowl or on an attractive platter to brighten
it up.

PESTO

1 cup moderately well-
packed basil leaves, well
rinsed and drained

⅓ cup olive oil

2 garlic cloves, chopped

¼ cup grated Parmesan
cheese

1 tablespoon unsalted
butter, softened

· ·

1 pound fresh or frozen
cheese tortellini

1 tablespoon pine nuts

Few sprigs fresh basil, for
garnish

Serves 4 as a main course

❶ To make the pesto: Combine the basil, olive oil,
and garlic in a blender or food processor and process until smooth. Scrape into a bowl, then stir in
the cheese and butter. (You can make this in
advance and refrigerate for 2 weeks.)

❷ Bring a large stockpot of water to a boil. Cook the
tortellini until tender but not mushy. Taste to be
certain the tortellini is done. Drain thoroughly in a
colander, then place in a serving bowl. Spoon on
the pesto *(see Note)* and toss very well. Sprinkle on
the pine nuts and toss again. Serve the salad at
room temperature with one or two sprigs of basil as
garnish.

☛*Note:* If the pesto is cold and firm, you can thin it
with a few drops of the hot pasta cooking water.

COLD ORIENTAL NOODLES WITH PEANUT SAUCE

*L*ike so many of life's delicacies, the flavors in this captivating sauce linger long after the thrill is gone!

1 pound spaghettini

4 tablespoons oriental sesame oil

. . . .

½ cup natural-style peanut butter

⅓ cup tamari soy sauce

3 tablespoons Chinese rice wine, *or* sherry

1 tablespoon water

1½ tablespoon rice vinegar, *or* other vinegar

1 tablespoon vegetable oil

1 tablespoon firmly packed light brown sugar

3 garlic cloves, minced

1 teaspoon minced fresh ginger

½ teaspoon crushed red pepper flakes (or less for a milder version)

. . . .

1 cucumber, peeled, cut lengthwise, seeded, and julienned

4 scallions, thinly sliced

Serves 4 as a main course

❶ Cook the spaghettini al dente. Drain and rinse under cold water. Drain very well again. With your hands, toss the noodles with 2 tablespoons of the sesame oil. Cover and chill until ready to combine with the peanut sauce, or up to 24 hours.

❷ To make the sauce, combine the remaining 2 tablespoons sesame oil with all the other ingredients except the cucumber and scallions. Beat until well mixed. The sauce can be kept in the refrigerator, covered, up to 24 hours before using.

❸ Just before serving, gently toss the noodles with the sauce, cucumbers, and half the scallions. Garnish with the remaining scallions.

ORZO AND VEGETABLE SALAD

*osef Oszuscik, an adven-
turous cook in a California monastery, gave me
the idea for this tasty salad. It has a light, creamy
dressing and a potpourri of Mediterranean flavors.
Great as a main course or side dish.*

1½ cups orzo (rice-shaped pasta)

1 medium zucchini, quartered lengthwise and thinly sliced

10 Kalamata (Greek) olives, pitted and sliced

4 scallions, thinly sliced

1 celery rib, thinly sliced

1 medium tomato, seeded and cubed

1 green or red bell pepper, seeded and finely diced

⅓ cup minced fresh parsley

⅓ cup olive oil

2 tablespoons red wine vinegar

3 garlic cloves, minced

1 teaspoon dried oregano

1 tablespoon minced fresh dill, *or* 1 teaspoon dried

¼ teaspoon salt

Freshly ground black pepper to taste

4 ounces (⅔ cup) crumbled feta cheese

2 tablespoons mayonnaise

Serves 4 as a main course

❶ Bring a large stockpot of water to a boil. Add the orzo and cook until tender but not mushy, 6 to 8 minutes. Drain in a colander and rinse under cold water. Drain again very thoroughly. Place in a large bowl.

❷ Stir in the zucchini, olives, scallions, celery, tomato, bell pepper, and parsley.

❸ In a small bowl, beat together the olive oil, vinegar, garlic, oregano, dill, salt, and pepper. Pour over the salad and toss to coat well. Sprinkle on the feta cheese and toss again. Spoon on the mayonnaise and gently toss to coat evenly. Chill at least 2 hours, then bring to room temperature before serving. This salad can be stored in the refrigerator up to 8 hours before serving.

MISO DRESSING

This creamy, tangy dressing is made for a crunchy lettuce such as Romaine.

3 tablespoons rice (white) miso, *or* barley (red) miso

2 garlic cloves, chopped

2 tablespoons apple cider vinegar, *or* red wine vinegar

1½ tablespoons oriental sesame oil

¾ cup vegetable oil

⅓ cup plus 1 tablespoon water

Makes 1½ cups

❶ Blend the miso, garlic, vinegar, and sesame oil in a blender or food processor until smooth.

❷ With the machine still running, very slowly pour in the oil. When the mixture has emulsified, slowly pour in the water and blend 10 seconds or so. The finished dressing should have a smooth, mayonnaiselike consistency. Scrape into a serving dish, cover, and chill until ready to use. The dressing can be kept refrigerated for up to 4 days.

☞*Note:* If by chance your dressing separates, try scraping the dressing into a bowl. Clean and dry the processor or blender, put 1 tablespoon cold water in the container, and turn on the machine. With the cover off, pour in 1 tablespoon of the dressing. Once incorporated, add another 1 tablespoon dressing. Repeat until all the dressing has been added. It should rebind to a thick, creamy consistency.

TAHINI SALAD DRESSING

*S*erve a crunchy lettuce such as romaine with this savory garlic- and lemon-spiked dressing, and garnish with sesame seeds.

⅔ cup tahini

2 garlic cloves, pressed

6 tablespoons fresh lemon juice

½ teaspoon salt

5 to 7 tablespoons water

Makes 1¼ cups

❶ In a medium bowl, beat the tahini, garlic, lemon juice, and salt together until smooth. Slowly beat in the water, using just the amount needed to give the dressing a nice pouring consistency. Let sit 20 minutes before serving. The dressing will thicken slightly. Leftovers can be stored in refrigerator up to 4 days.

MISO. This fermented soy food has a pastelike consistency and usually is diluted with water to make stocks, sauces, and dressings. A highly concentrated source of protein, vitamin B-12, and minerals, miso is devoid of cholesterol and low in fat. Generally speaking, the darker the color of miso, the stronger the flavor and the more intense the saltiness. White or yellow miso is sweet, creamy, and ideal for dishes requiring a light touch. Choose unpasteurized miso sold refrigerated in health food stores. The unpasteurized product is filled with lactobacillus bacteria and enzymes, which aid digestion.

CREAMY HERB VINAIGRETTE

This is a wonderful way to use leftover egg white; it makes this dressing thick and creamy, and the emulsion will hold together for a number of days. Serve this on romaine lettuce with a generous handful of Parmesan cheese, and top with croutons.

2 garlic cloves, chopped

1 cup olive oil

1 teaspoon Dijon mustard

1 tablespoon water

1 egg white

⅓ cup red wine vinegar

¼ teaspoon dried oregano

¼ teaspoon dried basil

Pinch dried marjoram

Salt to taste

Freshly ground black pepper to taste

Makes 1¾ cups

❶ Combine all the ingredients in a blender or food processor and process 15 seconds, or until the dressing binds and is smooth. Scrape into a pitcher or jar. If the dressing is too thick, stir in a bit of water to thin. Cover and chill until serving time. It will keep for up to 3 days.

DOUBLE SESAME DRESSING

*he dark, bewitching
flavor of sesame comes from both the seeds and
the oil in this dressing. It pairs especially well with
spinach salads and with lettuce-based salads that
have a handful of watercress or arugula tossed in.*

1 tablespoon sesame seeds

½ cup peanut oil *or*
vegetable oil

1½ tablespoons oriental
sesame oil

2½ tablespoons red wine
vinegar *or* cider vinegar

½ teaspoon tamari soy sauce

1 garlic clove, pressed

Salt to taste

Freshly ground black
pepper to taste

Makes ¾ cup

❶ Place the sesame seeds in a small saucepan over medium-high heat and toast until they begin to smoke and become fragrant, about 3 minutes. Shake the pan around while the seeds are cooking to toast them evenly. Pour the seeds into a small bowl and cool.

❷ Combine all of the remaining ingredients in a jar with a screw-on top, then pour in the sesame seeds. Shake vigorously and chill. This dressing can be kept in the refrigerator for up to 4 days.

CREAMY GARLIC DRESSING

*his pungent dressing
can enliven a salad of greens or serve as a marinade for cold blanched vegetables.*

½ cup mayonnaise

½ cup plain low-fat yogurt

2 garlic cloves, pressed

1 teaspoon Dijon mustard

2 tablespoons fresh lemon
juice

Makes about 1 cup

❶ In a bowl or glass measuring cup, beat the mayonnaise and yogurt together until smooth.

❷ Beat in the garlic, mustard, and lemon juice until blended. Cover and chill until ready to use, up to 4 days.

BLUE CHEESE VINAIGRETTE

*S*oft lettuces such as Boston or green- or red-leaf lettuce mixed with some watercress and red onion slivers pair well with this vinaigrette.

2 tablespoons red wine vinegar

1 tablespoon Dijon mustard

1 garlic clove, pressed

Salt to taste

Freshly ground black pepper to taste

Pinch sugar

6 tablespoons olive oil

½ cup (2 ounces) crumbled blue cheese

Makes ⅔ cup

❶ In a small bowl, thoroughly beat together the vinegar, mustard, garlic, salt, pepper, and sugar. Slowly beat in the olive oil, then stir in the blue cheese. Chill. Toss with the salad just before serving. This vinaigrette will keep, refrigerated, for up to 4 days.

SANDWICHES
AND
SPREADS

Vegetarians have clearly been at a disadvantage when lunchtime rolled around. Cold cuts and tuna, the staples of most nonvegetarian sandwiches, have always made sandwich making simple and effortless for meat eaters. But for vegetarians, sandwiches have been problematic.

The sandwiches presented here range from the sophisticated to the simple. A number of them, such as Provençal Eggplant and Tomato Sandwiches with Garlic Mayonnaise (page 105) and Vegetable Melt with Wasabi Mayonnaise (page 103), could make a satisfying and delicious supper.

Sandwich making invites improvisation; therefore, I hope these recipes will inspire you to invent your own combinations, expanding your lunch repertoire. Always work with high-quality ingredients: nicely textured breads; ripe, juicy tomatoes; fresh, crisp greens; good-quality mayonnaise and mustard; and thinly sliced, savory cheese. This will get you off to the right start.

MEDITERRANEAN VEGETABLE SANDWICH

he intoxicating flavors of the Mediterranean are wedded in this aromatic "stuffed" sandwich. French breads vary greatly in width and texture. For this sandwich a wide, soft loaf works best.

1 wide, soft loaf French bread, cut into 4 pieces

10 tablespoons fruity olive oil

4 garlic cloves, minced

Freshly ground black pepper to taste

1 teaspoon dried oregano

2 tablespoons minced fresh basil, *or* 1½ teaspoons dried

1 green bell pepper, thinly sliced into rings

1 small red onion, thinly sliced

2 large tomatoes, thickly sliced

10 ounces sliced provolone cheese (preferably smoked)

5 to 6 ounces (28 to 30) Kalamata (Greek) olives

Serves 4

❶ Slice each French bread section in half horizontally and pull some of the inner bread from each half-section to make a cavity. Drizzle an equal amount of olive oil on each half-section and spread it around with a knife to coat the bread. Sprinkle equal amounts of the garlic, black pepper, oregano, and basil on each piece of bread.

❷ Layer the bell pepper, onion, tomato, and provolone cheese in one half of each bread section.

❸ One at a time, place an olive on a cutting board and rest the flat side of a cutting knife on it. Thump it with the heel of your hand, the olive will split and the pit will fall out. Discard the pits and place the olives on the sandwich bottoms. Cover the sandwich with the remaining bread halves.

❹ Tightly wrap each sandwich with plastic wrap and let sit at least 1 hour, or up to 4 hours, before serving. Sandwiches can sit for 1 hour unrefrigerated, on in the refrigerator if longer. Return to room temperature before serving.

PITA BREAD STUFFED WITH GREEK SALAD

Serve this aromatic salad sandwich with black olives to nibble.

3 tablespoons olive oil

2 teaspoons red wine vinegar

1 teaspoon dried oregano

Freshly ground black pepper to taste

1 green bell pepper, cored and cut into 1-inch dice

1 cucumber, peeled, seeded, and cut into 1-inch dice

½ cup slivered red onion

¼ pound (about ¾ cup) feta cheese, cut into ½-inch cubes

12 cherry tomatoes, halved, *or* 2 small tomatoes, cubed

1½ cups diced romaine or iceberg lettuce

4 pita breads, halved

Serves 4

❶ In a large bowl, whisk together the olive oil, vinegar, oregano, and pepper. Stir in the bell pepper, cucumber, onion, feta cheese, tomatoes, and lettuce until coated.

❷ Heat the pita bread halves in a 350°F. oven until just heated through, then cool. (You can omit this step, but I find that it enhances the texture of the bread.) Stuff some salad in each pita half and serve immediately.

☛*Note:* You can prepare the salad mixture up to 30 minutes in advance, but don't combine with the dressing until just before serving.

PITA BREAD PIZZAS

ere is the most popular lunch in my house, served at least three times a week! These pizzas are excellent plain or dressed with a favorite topping such as sliced black olives, mushrooms, or red pepper flakes. I love the combination of mozzarella and Muenster cheese; mozzarella alone is too firm and stringy, and Muenster adds a wonderful creaminess.

The proportions in this recipe are for 6-inch pita. You can easily adjust the amounts if your bread is a different size.

4 6-inch pita breads

½ cup tomato sauce

¾ cup grated mozzarella cheese

¾ cup grated Muenster cheese

Toppings of your choice (optional)

Makes four 6-inch pizzas

❶ Preheat the broiler. Lay the pita breads on a baking sheet and lightly toast on both sides. (You don't want them brown, just hot through and barely toasted.)

❷ Remove the pan from the oven and place each pita concave side up so the sauce and cheese won't run down the edges. Evenly divide the sauce and spread it on top of each bread. Sprinkle on the cheeses and any toppings.

❸ Place the baking sheet under the broiler and cook until the cheese begins to bubble. At this point, I usually remove the pan and spread the cheese more evenly with a knife. Return to the broiler and cook another minute or so, or until the cheese begins to brown.

❹ Place the pizzas one by one on a cutting board and cut in half with a large knife. Serve immediately.

GREEK PIZZA

This is simplicity itself, yet very aromatic and flavorful. A good-quality, fruity olive oil can really stand out in this recipe. If you have some on hand, by all means use it lavishly.

4 6-inch pita breads

6 ounces (about 1¼ cups) crumbled feta cheese

1¼ teaspoons dried oregano

4 paper-thin slices onion, separated into rings

2 tablespoons fruity olive oil

Makes four 6-inch pizzas

❶ Preheat the broiler. Place the pita breads on a baking sheet concave sides up. Sprinkle the feta cheese on top of the bread. Sprinkle on the oregano, and top with the onion rings. Drizzle the olive oil over all.

❷ Broil 5 minutes, or until the cheese softens and the edges of the bread begin to brown. Place the pizzas on a cutting board and slice in half. Serve immediately.

TOFU "EGGLESS" SALAD

This sandwich filling is similar in taste, texture, and appearance to egg salad. Spread on a good-quality whole wheat bread and top with romaine lettuce for a delicious sandwich combination. You can also serve it on toasted French bread slices as an appetizer.

½ pound extra-firm or firm tofu, patted very dry

¼ teaspoon turmeric

2 tablespoons mayonnaise

1 tablespoon finely diced red onion

Fills 4 sandwiches

❶ Place the tofu in a medium bowl and mash it with a fork until crumbs the size of small peas are formed.

❷ Stir in the turmeric and mix well, then stir in the remaining ingredients. Let sit 30 minutes before using, or cover and chill for up to 24 hours.

WASABI. Wasabi is green horseradish that is sold in powdered form. When mixed with a few drops of water, it makes a paste that is used as a condiment in Japanese cooking. Wasabi's fiery flavor goes a long way, so only a small amount is needed to enliven a dish.

Wasabi can be purchased in health food stores, specialty food shops, and the oriental section of some supermarkets.

VEGETABLE MELT WITH *WASABI* MAYONNAISE

Almost any sautéed vegetable mixture will do on this open-faced sandwich. Just season it with tamari, sprinkle on Muenster cheese, broil until melted, and top with a generous spoonful of this spunky wasabi mayonnaise.

1 teaspoon *wasabi* powder (see opposite page)

3 tablespoons mayonnaise

1 tablespoon olive oil

12 ounces (4½ cups) sliced mushrooms

1 large red bell pepper, cored and cut into thin strips

1 bunch broccoli, cut into small pieces and stalks peeled (about 5 cups)

2 teaspoons tamari soy sauce

2 7-inch pita breads

1¼ cups grated Muenster cheese

Serves 4

❶ Mix the *wasabi* with about 1 teaspoon water, or just enough to make a paste the consistency of mustard. Let sit 10 minutes to develop the flavor. Place the mayonnaise in a small bowl and stir until smooth, then stir in the *wasabi* paste. Set aside.

❷ Heat the olive oil in a large skillet over medium-high heat. Add the mushrooms and sauté 5 minutes, tossing often. Stir in the bell pepper and broccoli, then sprinkle on about 1 tablespoon water. Cover and cook until the broccoli is crisp-tender, about 5 minutes.

❸ Remove the cover from the pan. If there is any water remaining, raise the heat to high to evaporate it. Stir the mixture frequently. Pour on the tamari and toss to coat. Remove from the heat.

❹ Preheat the broiler. Meanwhile, split the pitas in half to make 4 disks. Place them on a baking sheet, then spoon on the vegetable mixture. Sprinkle on the cheese, and broil until melted, about 3 minutes. Slip onto serving plates. Spoon an equal portion of the *wasabi* mayonnaise in the center of each sandwich, and let each person spread it.

VEGETABLE CREAM CHEESE SPREAD

Garlic and scallions spark this pretty, salmon-colored crunchy spread that will please the palates of children and adults alike. This spread is a good choice when sandwiches are to be transported because they will hold together well.

1 large carrot, peeled

8 ounces Neufchâtel or cream cheese, softened

1 small garlic clove, pressed or minced

Salt

Freshly ground black pepper to taste

½ cucumber

2 scallions, very thinly sliced

¼ cup finely diced green bell pepper

Fills 4 sandwiches

❶ Cut the carrot into chunks and mince in a blender or food processor. Scrape it into a medium bowl and thoroughly mix the cream cheese into it with a fork. Mix in the garlic, salt, and pepper.

❷ Peel the cucumber half, then cut it in half lengthwise. Scrape out the seeds and discard them. Cut the cucumber into thin strips and then into small dice.

❸ Stir the cucumber, scallions, and bell pepper into the cream cheese mixture.

☛*Note:* This spread will keep up to 3 days if well wrapped and refrigerated.

☛*Variations:* Spread on pumpernickel bread and top with lettuce or alfalfa sprouts and another slice of bread. Or spread on a toasted or untoasted bagel and serve open-faced.

PROVENÇAL EGGPLANT AND TOMATO SANDWICHES WITH GARLIC MAYONNAISE

¾ cup mayonnaise

1 medium eggplant, peeled and sliced into ½-inch-thick rounds

⅓ cup plus 2 tablespoons grated Parmesan cheese

1 teaspoon Dijon mustard

2 garlic cloves, minced

1 loaf crusty French or Italian bread, *or* 4 crusty sandwich rolls

2 medium tomatoes, sliced

Makes 4 sandwiches

❶ Preheat the broiler. Using a pastry brush and ¼ cup of the mayonnaise, brush a thin layer of mayonnaise on both sides of the eggplant slices. Dip the slices in the Parmesan cheese to coat. Place the slices in one layer on a baking sheet and broil on both sides until a rich golden brown and very tender, about 10 minutes. Let cool to room temperature. (If you want to do this step up to 24 hours in advance, cover and chill the cooled eggplant slices. Before serving, bring to room temperature.)

❷ Mix the remaining ½ cup mayonnaise with the mustard and garlic.

❸ Halve the bread lengthwise and then cut the entire loaf into 4 sections. Brush each side generously with the garlic mayonnaise, then layer the bottom half of each bread section with the eggplant and tomato slices. Top with the remaining bread.

TEMPEH HEROS

After the tempeh slices are sautéed, a drizzling of tamari gives them a deep, rich, roasted flavor somewhat reminiscent of bacon. Layered with lettuce, tomato, and Russian dressing, the result is a satisfying sandwich that could be served as a quick dinner.

10 ounces tempeh (see opposite page)

2 tablespoons vegetable oil

2 teaspoons tamari soy sauce

RUSSIAN DRESSING

¼ cup mayonnaise

2½ tablespoons ketchup

1½ tablespoons sweet relish (optional)

4 submarine or hero rolls

4 romaine lettuce leaves

8 tomato slices

4 red onion slices

Makes 4 sandwiches

❶ Cut the tempeh into 4 slices, then cut each piece in half crosswise to make 8 thin slices.

❷ Heat the oil in a large skillet. When it is hot, add the tempeh and fry until golden brown on both sides. Remove the tempeh to a platter, then drizzle about ⅛ teaspoon tamari on top of each slice and rub it in with your fingers (the tempeh will quickly absorb it). Turn over the slices and repeat. Let the slices cool to room temperature or until slightly warm.

❸ Mix the mayonnaise, ketchup, and relish together to make the Russian dressing. Slice each roll lengthwise to open. Generously spread both sides of each roll with the Russian dressing, then layer with the tempeh, lettuce, and sliced onion.

TEMPEH. Tempeh is a fermented soybean product made by mixing cooked soybeans with a rhizopus culture and pressing the mixture into flat cakes. It has a beanier flavor and texture than tofu, and, unlike tofu, contains vitamin B-12, the vitamin most likely to be absent from a vegetarian or vegan diet. Tempeh is very high in protein, rich in calcium and iron, low in fat, and free of cholesterol. In Indonesia, where it originated, and in the West, tempeh is always cooked before it is eaten.

Fried tempeh cubes have a crisp but tender texture, and are delicious mixed with vegetables and coated with a marinara sauce or a Chinese sweet-and-sour sauce. The black specks found in tempeh are spores of the rhizopus culture and are not a sign of spoilage. Spoiled tempeh will smell bad, feel slimy, and have pink, green, or yellow discolorations.

TEMPEH SPREAD SANDWICHES

The flavor of this spread is reminiscent of chicken salad and bacon. I like to serve it on hard rolls with lettuce and tomato, but it is also delicious on toasted French bread or crackers.

10 ounces tempeh (see page 107)

1 tablespoon vegetable oil

2 teaspoons tamari soy sauce

¼ cup mayonnaise, plus extra for the bread

1 scallion, thinly sliced

1 celery rib, finely chopped

⅛ teaspoon celery seed

3 hard sandwich rolls

Romaine or iceberg lettuce leaves

Tomato slices

Makes 3 sandwiches

❶ Finely chop the tempeh, then heat the oil in a large skillet over medium-high heat. Sauté the tempeh until golden all over, about 7 minutes.

❷ Scrape the tempeh into a medium bowl, then mash with a fork until it resembles large crumbs. Pour on the tamari and mix well. Let cool to room temperature. Stir in the mayonnaise, scallion, celery, and celery seed. Cover and chill at least 30 minutes.

❸ To make sandwiches, spread some mayonnaise on sliced hard rolls. Spoon on the tempeh spread, then top with lettuce and sliced tomatoes.

GINGERED TOFU PEANUT SPREAD

*S*erve this ultracreamy
spread as a sandwich filling and top with cucumber slices to provide a delicious contrast in
texture and filling.

½ pound firm or extra-firm
tofu, patted very dry

1 tablespoon tamari soy
sauce

⅔ cup natural-style peanut
butter

1 tablespoon lemon juice

1½ teaspoons minced fresh
ginger

1 garlic clove, minced

2 tablespoons water

Fills 6 sandwiches

❶ Put the tofu and tamari in a blender or food processor and puree until a smooth, thick paste forms.
Turn off the blender and scrape down the sides as
necessary. Scrape the tofu into a medium bowl.

❷ With a fork, vigorously beat in all of the remaining ingredients. Let sit 30 minutes at room temperature before serving. This spread will keep 3 days,
covered and refrigerated.

ASSORTED TEA SANDWICHES

*M*ake a platter of these
for your next party or get-together; they'll
disappear in a flash. The bread slices and fillings
are all different colors and look quite lovely
when artfully arranged.

CUCUMBER AND DILL SANDWICHES

1 large cucumber

¼ teaspoon salt

¼ cup mayonnaise

1 teaspoon minced fresh dill

10 slices whole wheat bread, crusts removed

1 teaspoon white vinegar

Freshly ground black pepper to taste

SCALLION CREAM CHEESE SANDWICHES

3 scallions, thinly sliced

¼ cup minced fresh parsley

4 tablespoons unsalted butter, softened

4 ounces cream cheese, softened

Freshly ground black pepper to taste

10 slices good-quality white bread, crusts removed

CURRIED EGG SALAD SANDWICHES

4 hard-boiled eggs, peeled

1½ tablespoons mayonnaise, plus extra for bread

¼ teaspoon curry powder

❶ To make the cucumber and dill sandwiches: Peel the cucumber, then cut in half lengthwise. With a spoon, scrape out the seeds and discard them. Cut the cucumber into paper-thin half-moon slices. Toss with salt in a bowl and let sit 15 minutes.

❷ Meanwhile, mix the mayonnaise with the dill and spread on each bread slice. Drain the cucumber slices on paper towels. Return them to the bowl and toss with the vinegar and black pepper. Arrange the cucumbers over half of the bread slices, then top with the remaining bread slices. Cut each sandwich into 4 squares. Arrange neatly in the center of a large platter.

❸ To make the scallion and cream cheese sandwiches: In the container of a blender or food processor, combine the scallions and parsley and process until very fine. Add the butter, cream cheese, and pepper and blend until the mixture turns green. Scrape into a bowl, then spread on half the bread slices. Top with the remaining slices, then cut each sandwich into 4 triangles. Arrange the triangles standing up, next to the cucumber sandwiches.

❹ To make the curried egg salad sandwiches: Mince the hard-boiled eggs. Mix with the mayonnaise, curry powder, celery, onion, salt, and pepper. Lightly spread mayonnaise on each bread slice.

1½ tablespoons very thinly sliced celery

1 tablespoon finely chopped onion

Salt to taste

Freshly ground black pepper to taste

10 slices good-quality pumpernickel bread, crusts removed

. . . .

Fresh parsley and dill sprigs or nasturtiums, for garnish

Makes 60 tea sandwiches

Spread the egg salad on half the slices, then top with the remaining slices. Cut the sandwiches into 4 triangles. Place these triangles, standing up, on the other side of the cucumber sandwiches.

❺ Cover the sandwich platter with a slightly damp towel and plastic wrap. Chill until serving time. Garnish the platter with parsley and dill sprigs or nasturtiums.

GARLIC AND HERB TOFU SPREAD

ere's a richly flavored, smooth spread that is very low in fat and calories. This has become my favorite quick lunch, especially if I've overindulged the night before!

½ pound firm tofu, patted dry

1 garlic clove, pressed

2 teaspoons tamari soy sauce

¼ teaspoon dried basil

¼ teaspoon dried oregano

¼ teaspoon minced fresh dill

Fills 3 sandwiches

❶ Place the tofu, garlic, and tamari in a blender or food processor and blend until smooth. Turn off the machine and scrape down the sides as necessary. Scrape the spread into a bowl.

❷ Stir in the herbs, then cover and chill 30 minutes. Spread will keep 3 days in the refrigerator.

☛*Variations:* Spread between 2 slices of bread and top with sliced cucumbers and sprouts or lettuce. Or fill pita bread halves with raw vegetables and top with the spread.

ENTREES

PASTA PRONTO

Pasta has become the shining member of the complex-carbohydrate family. Because complex carbohydrates are metabolized slowly, they curb the appetite and have been singled out as the best source of fuel for the body. In addition, complex carbohydrates (grains, vegetables, legumes, and fruits) have not been linked to any fatal diseases, as have fats and sugar.

Pasta is one of the most versatile foods known to man. It can be prepared in limitless ways and is one of the most satisfying foods to eat. For vegetarians, pasta offers the means to create countless dishes, from the simple to the elegant.

The only drawback to many pasta dishes is the heavy reliance on rich sauces. Here, I have kept the use of cream, butter, and olive oil to a minimum without sacrificing flavor and consistency. If you are serving a pasta dish with cream in the sauce, balance the remainder of the meal by serving a light salad and a low-fat dessert.

Always cook pasta al dente, that is, tender yet slightly chewy to the bite. Overcooked pasta becomes mushy and doesn't react well with sauce. Although dried pasta has cooking instructions on the package, it is best to taste a piece to test for doneness, then drain it thoroughly in a colander before mixing with a sauce. If you anticipate that your pasta will be done before you are ready to serve it, try the following trick: A few minutes before the pasta reaches the desired degree of doneness, remove the pot from the heat and let the pasta sit in the hot water until you are ready to serve. You'll probably have about 7 minutes leeway, since the pasta will still be cooking in the hot water, but at a much slower rate.

CAPELLINI WITH TOMATO PESTO

When I want to make an ultraquick pasta dish that will be a surefire winner, I choose this favorite recipe. The assertive tomato-based sauce is richly infused with garlic, basil, and olive oil, and like other pestos, it clings doggedly to the pasta. You won't be satisfied with traditional marinara sauce once you've tried this tomato pesto.

⅓ cup pine nuts

6 ounce can good-quality tomato paste

½ cup minced fresh parsley

¼ cup finely chopped fresh basil, *or* 2 teaspoons dried

½ cup olive oil

½ cup grated Parmesan cheese

2 garlic cloves, pressed or minced

½ teaspoon salt

Freshly ground black pepper to taste

1 pound capellini, *or* vermicelli or spaghettini

Serves 4

❶ Lightly toast the pine nuts in a 350°F. oven until golden, about 5 minutes.

❷ To make the sauce, combine the pine nuts with all the remaining ingredients except the pasta in a medium bowl. (This step may be completed up to 24 hours in advance, covered, and chilled. Bring to room temperature before mixing it with the pasta.)

❸ Bring a 6-quart pot of water to a boil. Add the pasta and cook until al dente. Before draining the pasta, beat 2 tablespoons of the boiling pasta water into the sauce. Drain the pasta and return it to the pot or drop it into a large bowl. Spoon on the sauce and toss quickly. Serve immediately.

TORTELLINI WITH SOUR CREAM SAUCE

A strikingly pretty presentation: Tortellini coated with a simple sour cream sauce is topped with a vivid mixture of bright-red diced tomatoes and green scallion slices.

1 pound fresh or frozen cheese tortellini

2 teaspoons unsalted butter

4 to 6 scallions, thinly sliced

2 medium tomatoes, cored, seeded, and diced

⅔ cup sour cream

2 tablespoons grated Parmesan cheese

½ teaspoon salt

Freshly ground black pepper to taste

Serves 4

❶ Bring a large pot of water to a boil and cook the tortellini until tender but not mushy. (It's a good idea to taste one to judge accurately.)

❷ Meanwhile, melt the butter in a medium skillet, add the scallions and tomatoes, and sauté 2 minutes, or until the vegetables are hot throughout. Set aside.

❸ In a small bowl mix together the sour cream, Parmesan cheese, salt, and pepper.

❹ Drain the tortellini thoroughly, then return it to the pot. Pour on the sour cream mixture and toss quickly to coat. Spoon the tortellini onto serving plates, and spoon some of the tomato mixture in the center of each serving.

VEGETABLE LO MEIN

*find the following
unconventional method an easy and relaxing
alternative to stir-frying pasta.*

½ pound linguine *or*
spaghettini

1 tablespoon oriental sesame
oil

2 tablespoons tamari soy
sauce

VEGETABLES

3 tablespoons vegetable oil

1 pound extra-firm or firm
tofu, cut into ½-inch cubes
and patted very dry

2 garlic cloves, minced

1 teaspoon minced fresh
ginger

4½ cups (about 12 ounces)
thinly sliced mushrooms

2 scallions, thinly sliced

1 tablespoon tamari soy
sauce

2 teaspoons oriental sesame
oil

Serves 3 to 4

❶ Cook the pasta al dente in a large pot of boiling water. The noodles should remain a little chewy in texture. Drain very well in a colander. Mix the sesame oil and soy sauce together, pour over the noodles, and toss to coat. Place in a baking dish and cover with foil. Keep warm in a 300°F. oven while stir-frying the vegetables. (The noodles can be prepared up to 24 hours in advance and chilled. To reheat, sprinkle with 2 tablespoons of water, then cover and reheat in a 300°F. oven till hot, about 15 minutes.)

❷ In a wok or large skillet, heat 2 tablespoons of the oil over high heat until hot but not smoking. Add the tofu and stir-fry until golden all over. Remove to a platter. Reduce the heat to medium and add the remaining 1 tablespoon of the oil. Stir-fry the garlic and ginger 30 seconds. Add the mushrooms and stir-fry until brown and juicy, about 7 minutes. Return the tofu to the pan and toss. Add the scallions and stir-fry 2 minutes. Sprinkle on the soy sauce and sesame oil and toss again.

❸ Remove the noodles from the oven. Spoon on the vegetable mixture and toss thoroughly. Serve immediately, or cover and keep warm in the oven for up to 20 minutes.

ULTRAQUICK LASAGNA

Preparing this lasagna takes just 10 minutes because the noodles are not precooked. Raw noodles are layered with ricotta and mozzarella cheeses and surrounded with a thin tomato-wine sauce that cooks the noodles until tender. It's delicious and it works!

1 32-ounce jar (4 cups) tomato sauce

1 garlic clove, pressed

½ cup dry red wine

1½ cups water

1 teaspoon dried oregano

2 large eggs

2 cups (about 15 ounces) part-skim ricotta cheese

¼ cup grated Parmesan cheese

¼ teaspoon freshly ground nutmeg

1 pound uncooked lasagna

1 pound (about 5 cups) grated mozzarella cheese

Serves 6

❶ Preheat the oven to 350°F. In a large bowl, combine the tomato sauce, garlic, wine, water, and oregano.

❷ In a medium bowl, beat the eggs. Beat in the ricotta and Parmesan cheeses and the nutmeg.

❸ Pour a generous amount of sauce on the bottom of a 9 × 13-inch pan or baking dish, or on the bottoms of 2 smaller baking dishes. (You must give the lasagna enough room to swell during cooking.) Alternating the lasagna, sauce, ricotta mixture, and mozzarella, make about three layers, ending with the mozzarella.

❹ Cover the pan(s) tightly with aluminum foil. (The lasagna may be prepared to this point and refrigerated up to 24 hours in advance. Bring to room temperature before baking.) Bake 1 hour, remove the foil, and continue baking 15 minutes, or until the sauce has thickened and the noodles are tender. Let sit 10 minutes before cutting.

LINGUINE WITH CAULIFLOWER IN A TOMATO CREAM SAUCE

Tomato cream is one of the most seductive pasta sauces. Combined with cauliflower and hot peppers, it transforms pasta into a truly elegant creation.

1 pound linguine

2 tablespoons olive oil

4 garlic cloves, minced

¼ teaspoon crushed red pepper flakes

1 large cauliflower, cut into small flowerets (about 7 cups)

1 cup tomato puree

1 cup light cream, *or* ½ cup heavy cream mixed with ½ cup milk

¼ teaspoon freshly ground nutmeg

½ teaspoon salt

Freshly ground black pepper to taste

¼ cup minced fresh parsley

Grated Parmesan cheese

Serves 4

❶ Bring a large stockpot of water to a boil. Drop in the linguine and cook until al dente.

❷ Meanwhile, heat the olive oil in a large skillet over medium heat. Add the garlic and red pepper flakes and cook 2 minutes. Do not let the garlic brown. Stir in the cauliflower and toss to coat well. Pour in ⅓ cup water and cover the pan. Cook 10 minutes, or until the cauliflower is tender but not mushy. Remove the cover and toss occasionally.

❸ Mix together the tomato puree, cream, nutmeg, salt, and pepper. Pour over the cauliflower and toss well. Bring to a boil, then turn off the heat.

❹ Drain the linguine in a colander. Place some linguine on each serving plate. Spoon on the sauce, then garnish with the minced parsley. Pass the Parmesan cheese at the table.

ZITI WITH BROCCOLI AND RICOTTA SAUCE

*P*art-skim ricotta
**cheese is the base for this creamy sauce, making it
relatively low in fat.**

½ pound ziti, *or penne,
rigatoni, or rotini*

1 tablespoon unsalted butter

1 tablespoon olive oil

3 garlic cloves, minced

⅛ teaspoon crushed red
pepper flakes

3 scallions, thinly sliced

1 bunch broccoli, stalks
peeled and cut into small
pieces (about 5 cups)

1 cup part-skim ricotta
cheese, at room temperature

¼ cup milk

¼ cup grated Parmesan
cheese

¼ teaspoon dried basil

¼ teaspoon dried oregano

¼ teaspoon salt

Freshly ground black
pepper to taste

Serves 2 to 3

❶ Bring a large pot of water to a boil, then cook the ziti until al dente, about 15 minutes.

❷ Meanwhile, heat the butter and olive oil in a large skillet over medium heat. Add the garlic, red pepper flakes, and scallions; sauté 2 minutes, stirring frequently. Add the broccoli, toss, then add a few tablespoons of water. Cover the pan and cook just until the broccoli is tender but still bright green, about 5 minutes. Keep warm over low heat.

❸ In a medium bowl beat together the ricotta, milk, Parmesan, basil, oregano, salt, and pepper, along with 2 tablespoons of the boiling pasta water.

❹ Drain the ziti in a colander. Place in a large serving bowl or return to the pot. Stir in the ricotta mixture to coat, then toss with the broccoli. Serve immediately.

RAVIOLI WITH GARLIC, PEPPERS, AND TOMATOES

Olive oil, garlic, bell pepper strips, and diced tomatoes combine to make a spicy, chunky sauce that suits the bulky texture of ravioli perfectly.

1 pound fresh or frozen cheese ravioli

¼ cup olive oil

3 garlic cloves, minced

¼ teaspoon crushed red pepper flakes

3 medium green bell peppers, cored and cut into ½-inch strips

3 medium tomatoes, cored, seeded, and diced

½ teaspoon dried oregano

¼ teaspoon dried thyme

Salt to taste

Freshly ground black pepper to taste

Grated Parmesan cheese

Serves 4

❶ Bring a large pot of water to a boil and cook the ravioli until tender.

❷ Meanwhile, make the sauce. In a large skillet, heat the olive oil over medium heat. Add the garlic and the red pepper flakes and cook 2 minutes. Do not let the garlic brown.

❸ Toss in the pepper strips and sauté, stirring often, for 10 minutes, or until the peppers are almost tender. Raise the heat to medium-high. Add the tomatoes, oregano, thyme, salt, and pepper and cook 5 minutes more, or until the peppers are tender and the tomatoes are heated through. (The tomatoes will have rendered their juices and made a light sauce.)

❹ Drain the ravioli and return to the pot or place in a large pasta serving bowl. Spoon on the sauce and toss lightly. Pass the Parmesan cheese at the table.

BABY RAVIOLI WITH CREAM, MUSHROOMS, AND PEAS

he small ravioli known as raviolini are available in many supermarkets in the frozen-foods section. If you cannot find them, substitute cheese tortellini or regular-size ravioli.

1 pound fresh or frozen cheese raviolini

2 tablespoons olive oil

4½ cups (about 12 ounces) fresh mushrooms, sliced

2 cups (about 1 pound) frozen peas

½ cup heavy cream

Salt to taste

Freshly ground black pepper to taste

2 tablespoons unsalted butter, cut into bits

Grated Parmesan cheese

Serves 4

❶ In a large stockpot, cook the raviolini in boiling water until tender, about 10 to 15 minutes.

❷ Meanwhile, make the sauce. In a large skillet, heat the olive oil over medium heat. Add the mushrooms and cook until brown and juices evaporate, about 10 minutes. Add the peas and cook 3 minutes more, or until heated through. Stir in the cream and bring to a boil. Season with salt and pepper, then remove from the heat.

❸ Drain the ravioli thoroughly. Meanwhile, melt the butter in the stockpot, then return the ravioli to the pot and toss to coat. Pour on the sauce and heat until bubbly, about 1 minute. Serve with some Parmesan cheese sprinkled on each serving.

PENNE WITH SPINACH AND CHICK-PEAS IN GARLIC SAUCE

A light, flavorful way to serve pasta that is also nutritious and low in fat. This sauce goes well with a short, tubular pasta, so if you cannot get penne, or mostaccioli, try ziti, rigatoni, or rotini (short spirals).

1 10-ounce package loose fresh spinach, *or* 1 10-ounce package frozen chopped spinach, thawed

1 pound *penne* or *mostaccioli* (short, quill-shaped pasta)

⅓ cup olive oil

6 garlic cloves, minced

¼ teaspoon crushed red pepper flakes

2 medium tomatoes, cored, seeded, and cut into ½-inch dice

2 cups freshly cooked chick-peas (see page 161), *or* 1 15-ounce can chick-peas, rinsed and drained

¼ teaspoon salt

¼ cup grated Parmesan cheese

Serves 4

❶ Clean the fresh spinach and discard the stems. Place the spinach in a large skillet with just the water that clings to it, cover, and cook over medium heat just until wilted, about 5 minutes. Drain, cool, then squeeze dry with your hands. (If you are using frozen spinach, just squeeze out all of the moisture with your hands.) Set aside.

❷ Bring a 6-quart pot of water to a boil and add the *penne*. Cook until al dente, 12 to 15 minutes.

❸ Meanwhile, make the sauce. Heat the olive oil in a large skillet over medium heat. Add the garlic and red pepper flakes and cook 2 minutes. Add the tomatoes and chick-peas and cook 2 minutes more. Add the spinach, salt, and ¼ cup of the boiling pasta water and stir well. Cook until heated through, about 3 minutes.

❹ When the pasta is done, drain it thoroughly in a colander. Return it to the pot or put it in a large serving bowl. Spoon on the sauce and toss well. Sprinkle on the Parmesan cheese, toss again, and serve with additional cheese to pass at the table.

SPAGHETTINI WITH CRUMBLED BLUE CHEESE

This is simplicity itself,
yet intensely flavorful and appealing.

1 pound spaghettini

3 tablespoons unsalted butter

¼ cup olive oil

1 cup minced fresh parsley

1 cup (about 4 ounces) crumbled blue cheese

Serves 4

❶ Cook the spaghettini until al dente in a large pot of boiling water.

❷ Meanwhile, melt the butter with the olive oil in a small saucepan. Remove from the heat and stir in the parsley.

❸ Drain the spaghettini and place in a large bowl. Pour on the parsley sauce and toss very well. Sprinkle on the crumbled blue cheese and toss again. Serve immediately.

FETTUCCINE MARGHERITA

After having this dish in Montreal one summer, the lingering memory of the sauce followed me home. I experimented with this dish until I captured the original's earthy blend of mushrooms, tangy tomatoes, and silky cream. A superb pasta dish with great panache.

1 pound fettuccine

2 tablespoons olive oil

2 tablespoons unsalted butter

12 ounces (about 4½ cups) sliced mushrooms

4 garlic cloves, minced

¼ teaspoon crushed red pepper flakes

1 28-ounce can imported plum tomatoes, well drained and chopped

¼ cup white wine

½ cup heavy cream

½ teaspoon salt

⅓ cup grated Parmesan cheese

Serves 4

❶ Cook the fettuccine until al dente in a large pot of boiling water.

❷ Meanwhile, in a large skillet heat the olive oil and butter over medium-high heat. Add the mushrooms and sauté until they brown and the juices begin to evaporate, about 7 minutes.

❸ Add the garlic and red pepper and cook for 2 minutes, stirring frequently. Add the tomatoes and wine and boil 2 minutes, stirring often. Add the cream and salt and boil 1 minute.

❹ Drain the fettuccine thoroughly. Return to the pot or place in a large bowl, then pour on the sauce and sprinkle on the Parmesan cheese. Toss quickly and serve immediately.

FETTUCCINE WITH ASPARAGUS IN LEMON CREAM SAUCE

A rich—but not too rich—
way to celebrate spring's asparagus crop.

¾ pound fettuccine

1 tablespoon olive oil

2 garlic cloves, minced

¾ pound asparagus, stalks peeled and cut into 1-inch pieces

½ cup heavy cream

½ cup milk

Grated rind of 1 lemon

¼ teaspoon freshly grated nutmeg

½ teaspoon salt

Freshly ground black pepper to taste

⅓ cup grated Parmesan cheese

Serves 4

❶ Cook the fettuccine until al dente in a large pot of boiling water.

❷ Meanwhile, heat the oil in a large skillet over medium heat. Add the garlic and asparagus and sauté, tossing constantly, 2 minutes. Pour in about 2 tablespoons water and cover the pan. Cook until the asparagus are just tender, about 5 minutes. Combine the cream, milk, lemon rind, nutmeg, salt, and pepper. Pour over the asparagus and bring to a boil.

❸ Drain the fettuccine and return to the pot. Pour on the asparagus sauce, toss, and stir in the Parmesan cheese. Serve immediately.

SOBA WITH BROCCOLI AND *WASABI*

*S*oba (buckwheat noo-
dles) is especially suited to being served in
broth, Japanese fashion. Here, wasabi, a Japanese
green horseradish paste, is used to spike the
broth and give it a wonderful pungency.
　This dish is particularly light and contains
almost no fat, so it serves two, allowing two bowlfuls per person.

1 bunch broccoli, stalks
peeled and cut into small
pieces (about 5 cups)

8 ounces *soba* (buckwheat
noodles)

1 teaspoon *wasabi* powder
(see page 102)

1¾ cups vegetable stock (*see
Note*)

3 tablespoons *mirin* (sweet
sake) *or* pale dry sherry

3 tablespoons tamari soy
sauce

2 scallions, very thinly
sliced

Serves 2

❶ Bring a large stockpot of water to a boil. Drop in the broccoli, cover the pot, and cook 5 minutes, or until the broccoli is tender but still bright green. Remove with a slotted spoon and set aside.

❷ Let the water return to a rapid boil. Drop in the *soba* and cook until tender, about 10 minutes.

❸ Mix the *wasabi* and 1 teaspoon water together in a small dish (the resulting paste should have the consistency of smooth mustard; add a few more drops of water if necessary). Let sit 10 minutes to develop the flavor.

❹ While the *soba* is cooking, combine the stock, *mirin* or sherry, and tamari in a medium saucepan and bring to a boil.

❺ Drain the *soba* in a colander. Divide between 2 large bowls or 4 medium bowls. Place equal amounts of broccoli on top of each bowlful. Pour boiling stock into each bowl. Sprinkle on the scallions. Serve with the *wasabi* paste at the table, to spoon on as desired.

☞*Note:* Vegetable stock can be made with powdered vegetable stock base, available at health food stores.

PASTA FRITTATA

I'm indebted to Marcella
Hazan, noted Italian cookbook author, for the
marvelous idea of using leftover pasta in a frittata. I have become so enamored of this dish that
I hope family or guests don't finish all the pasta
so I can make this frittata the following evening.

For the filling, you can use plain spaghetti that
has been coated with butter, parsley, and cheese.
Elaborate preparations such as Fettuccine
Margherita (page 126) or Capellini with Tomato
Pesto (page 116) will be even more savory.
Improvisation is the key. This is the type of "pie"
that is rarely the same twice but is always good.
Serve it with Green Bean Salad with Lemon, Dill,
and Feta Cheese (page 178), a colorful side dish.

5 large eggs

⅓ cup grated Parmesan
cheese

¼ cup milk

4 cups cooked pasta

¼ teaspoon salt

Freshly ground black
pepper to taste

½ tablespoon unsalted
butter

Serves 3 to 4

❶ Preheat the oven to 350°F. Butter a pie plate and
set it aside.

❷ Beat the eggs in a large bowl until well mixed.
Stir in all of the remaining ingredients except the
butter. Pour the mixture into the pie plate. Cut the
butter into bits and distribute all over the top.

❸ Bake 10 minutes, then remove from the oven and
very lightly stir the mixture. Return to the oven and
bake an additional 10 to 15 minutes, or until a knife
inserted in the center comes out almost dry. Cut
into wedges and serve immediately.

PASTA AND VEGETABLE GRATIN

This baked pasta dish with a thin cheese sauce is much lighter than traditional macaroni and cheese and, to my mind, more appetizing. You can prepare much of this in advance, but don't pour on the sauce until you are ready to bake the gratin.

8 ounces (2 to 3 cups) *rotini*, macaroni, or ziti

1 medium yellow squash, cut into ½-inch dice

1 small red bell pepper, finely diced

2 scallions, thinly sliced

1 cup grated extra-sharp cheddar cheese

1 tablespoon unsalted butter

1 tablespoon unbleached flour

2¼ cups low-fat milk

¼ cup grated Parmesan cheese

⅛ teaspoon freshly grated nutmeg

¼ teaspoon dried dill

½ teaspoon salt

Freshly ground black pepper to taste

2 tablespoons bread crumbs

Serves 4

❶ Cook the *rotini* until al dente in a large pot of boiling water. Drain in a colander, then rinse under cold running water and drain again very thoroughly. Pour the pasta into a shallow dish such as a 2-quart oval gratin or a 12 × 7 × 2-inch baking dish.

❷ Stir in the yellow squash, red pepper, and scallions. Sprinkle on the cheddar cheese and lightly mix.

❸ Preheat the oven to 400°F. To make the sauce, melt the butter in a medium saucepan over medium heat. Whisk in the flour and let bubble, whisking constantly, until it begins to turn beige. Immediately whisk in the milk, and bring to a boil, whisking constantly. Remove from the heat and whisk in the Parmesan cheese, nutmeg, dill, salt, and pepper.

❹ Pour the sauce over the pasta mixture and toss lightly. Sprinkle on the bread crumbs. Bake 30 minutes, or until bubbly and brown on top.

GREAT GRAINS

With so much attention turned toward the importance of fiber in our diets, grains cookery has gained a new prominence. Although side dishes such as rice and bulghur pilafs have been around for some time, the use of grains in main courses has been less common.

Once you taste the delicious entrées in this chapter, you'll want to make grains a regular part of your diet. They are economical; highly nutritious, providing protein, vitamins, and much-needed fiber; and satisfying.

Many of the recipes in this chapter are low in fat and therefore a good choice if you have been indulging in rich foods recently. Because these entrées are complete in themselves, all you'll need is a fresh green salad to round off your meal.

BAKED STUFFED TOMATOES WITH COUSCOUS, PEAS, AND FETA CHEESE

A choice dish at the end *of the summer when fat, juicy tomatoes are abundant. Serve this with a green salad and French bread.*

4 large tomatoes

1 cup couscous

1½ cups boiling water

¼ cup plus 1 tablespoon olive oil

3 garlic cloves, minced

1 cup frozen peas, thawed

½ cup grated Parmesan cheese

1 cup (about 5 ounces) crumbled feta cheese

¼ cup minced fresh parsley

½ teaspoon dried oregano

Freshly ground black pepper to taste

Serves 4

❶ Slice the tomatoes in half horizontally. With a teaspoon, scoop out the pulp and seeds and discard. Drain the tomatoes upside down for 30 minutes.

❷ Meanwhile, make the stuffing. Place the couscous in a large bowl and stir in the boiling water. Cover and let sit 10 minutes. Preheat the oven to 375°F. Spread one tablespoon of the olive oil on the bottom of a large, shallow 2½-quart baking dish such as a 10 × 10 × 2-inch or other baking dish.

❸ In a small pan, heat the remaining ¼ cup of the olive oil and sauté the garlic until barely golden. Don't let it brown. Fluff the couscous with a fork and stir in the olive oil and garlic mixture and all the remaining ingredients.

❹ Divide the stuffing evenly among the tomato shells, pressing it in firmly. Bake 30 minutes. Pour the accumulated juices over the top when serving.

VEGETABLE COUSCOUS

A colorful medley of vegetables in a spicy sauce tops a mound of delicate couscous.

2 tablespoons olive oil

2 garlic cloves, minced

1 medium onion, diced

2 teaspoons ground cumin

½ teaspoon turmeric

1 teaspoon paprika

⅛ teaspoon cayenne pepper

2 medium zucchini, cut into ½-inch cubes

1 15-ounce can chick-peas, rinsed and drained, *or* 2 cups freshly cooked chick-peas (page 161)

1 16-ounce can tomatoes, finely chopped, with their juice

½ cup raisins

1½ cups vegetable stock *(see Note)*

½ teaspoon salt

2 tablespoons unsalted butter

1 cup couscous

Serves 3 to 4

❶ Heat the olive oil in a large skillet over medium-high heat. Add the garlic and onion and sauté 2 minutes. Sprinkle in the cumin, turmeric, paprika, and cayenne and cook 2 minutes more, stirring often.

❷ Stir in the zucchini, chick-peas, tomatoes, and raisins. Cover the pan and lower the heat to medium. Cook, stirring occasionally, until the zucchini is tender, about 10 minutes. (The juices should be thickened at this point. If they are not, remove the cover and boil a few minutes until thick.) You may prepare the dish to this point up to 8 hours in advance (cover and refrigerate, and reheat before proceeding with step 3).

❸ Meanwhile, prepare the couscous. Bring the stock, salt, and butter to a boil. Stir in the couscous, cover, remove from the heat, and let sit 5 minutes, or for up to 20 minutes. Fluff with a fork before serving.

❹ Serve the couscous with the vegetable mixture mounded in the center.

☛*Note:* Vegetable stock can be made with powdered vegetable stock base, available at health food stores.

BAKED COUSCOUS WITH SPINACH AND PINE NUTS

The fresh spinach in this garlic- and basil-scented concoction retains its vivid color and has a delightful texture because it is baked only for a short time. The entire dish can be assembled up to 24 hours in advance and is particularly good served with hot, crusty bread.

1 cup couscous

1½ cups boiling vegetable stock *(see Note,* page 133), *or* water

½ teaspoon salt

¼ cup olive oil

3 garlic cloves, minced

1 large onion, diced

1 28-ounce can tomatoes, chopped and drained (reserve ⅓ cup juice)

1½ tablespoons minced fresh basil, *or* 1 teaspoon dried

⅓ cup pine nuts

5 cups (about 5 ounces) loosely packed fresh spinach, stems removed and leaves torn into small pieces

Freshly ground black pepper to taste

1 cup grated Muenster cheese

Serves 4

❶ Combine the couscous, boiling stock or water, and salt in a large bowl; cover with a plate. Let sit 5 minutes, then fluff with a fork.

❷ Preheat the oven to 375°F. Heat the olive oil in a large skillet over medium heat. Sauté the garlic and onion 10 minutes, or until tender. Add the drained tomatoes and cook 10 minutes more, stirring frequently.

❸ Stir the tomato mixture into the couscous and mix in the reserved tomato juice, basil, pine nuts, raw spinach, and pepper.

❹ Spread half the couscous mixture in a 12 × 7 × 2-inch or other shallow (2½-quart) baking dish. Sprinkle on the cheese, then top with the remaining couscous. Cover the dish with foil and bake 25 minutes, or until hot and bubbly.

CURRIED BULGHUR WITH CHICK-PEAS AND VEGETABLES

*S*erve this with plain yogurt to provide a contrasting flavor and texture.

1½ cups bulghur

3 tablespoons vegetable oil

3 large scallions, thinly sliced, white and green parts separated

1 teaspoon turmeric

2 teaspoons ground coriander

1 tablespoon ground cumin

⅛ teaspoon ground cloves *or* allspice

¼ teaspoon cayenne pepper, or to taste

2 cups freshly cooked chick-peas (page 161), or 1 15-ounce can chick-peas, rinsed and drained

2 medium carrots, grated

1 16-ounce can plum tomatoes, seeded, well drained, and diced

1 tablespoon tamari soy sauce

Serves 4

❶ Rinse the bulghur in a sieve. Put the bulghur in a medium bowl and cover with boiling water by 2 inches. Soak uncovered for 30 minutes, or until tender when tasted. Drain thoroughly by spooning batches into a sieve and pressing out all of the liquid with the back of a spoon. Or put batches of the bulghur in a cotton kitchen towel or piece of cheesecloth and squeeze out the liquid. As the batches are completed put them in another medium bowl.

❷ Heat the oil in a large skillet over medium heat. Add the white parts of the scallions and sauté 3 minutes, tossing often.

❸ Sprinkle on the turmeric, coriander, cumin, cloves, and cayenne and cook 1 minute, stirring frequently. Add the drained chick-peas, the carrots, and the drained diced tomatoes, toss to mix, and cook 2 minutes.

❹ Stir in the drained bulghur, the green tops of the scallions, and the tamari and mix thoroughly. Cook, tossing occasionally, 10 minutes or until piping hot.

POLENTA WITH SPICY EGGPLANT SAUCE

*S*immering eggplant in
this tasty sauce rather than frying it reduces the
amount of fat needed and cuts down on time
spent in front of the stove. Here, the eggplant
sauce is spooned onto slices of slightly firm
polenta to make a colorful and substantial dish.

SAUCE

3 tablespoons olive oil

3 garlic cloves, minced

⅛ to ¼ teaspoon crushed
red pepper flakes

1 28-ounce can plum
tomatoes, roughly chopped,
with their juice

1 tablespoon tomato paste

2 teaspoons red wine
vinegar

½ teaspoon salt

Freshly ground black
pepper to taste

1 medium eggplant, peeled
and cut into ½-inch dice

1 green bell pepper, diced

. . . .

1¼ cups cornmeal

3½ cups water

½ teaspoon salt

1 tablespoon unsalted butter

¼ cup grated Parmesan
cheese

Minced fresh parsley

Serves 4 to 6

❶ To make the sauce, heat the olive oil in a large
skillet over medium heat. Add the garlic and red
pepper flakes and cook 30 seconds. Do not let the
garlic brown. Stir in the tomatoes and their juice.
Mix the tomato paste with the vinegar, stir it in,
then stir in the salt and pepper. Bring to a boil.

❷ Add the eggplant and cover the pan. Cook 10 minutes, stirring occasionally. Add the bell pepper,
cover again, and cook 10 minutes more, or until the
eggplant and pepper are tender. If the sauce is
watery, remove the cover and boil a few minutes
more until thickened. Keep warm while making the
polenta. (The recipe may be prepared up to 24
hours in advance to this point and the sauce
chilled. If too thick when reheated, add a few tablespoons water.)

❸ To make the polenta, combine the cornmeal,
water, and salt in a medium heavy saucepan. Place
over medium-high heat and bring to a boil, whisking often. When the cornmeal mixture begins to
boil, whisk constantly until the polenta is the consistency of mashed potatoes and begins to pull away
from the pot.

❹ Remove from the heat and stir in the butter and

cheese. Pour onto an oiled platter or large cutting board (about 10 × 8 inches) and let sit 20 minutes, or until firm enough to cut into 3-inch squares.

❺ Place the polenta squares on serving plates and spoon piping hot eggplant sauce over them. Garnish with parsley.

☛*Note:* Leftover polenta squares can be refrigerated up to 4 days, then reheated in the oven when needed.

CHEESE POLENTA

Here is a variation of a polenta dish created by my friend, cookbook author Richard Sax. If you are not familiar with polenta (boiled cornmeal), choose this recipe to make its acquaintance. It has a wonderfully cheesy, creamy consistency, and you'll find that you want to have cornmeal on hand to put this together at a moment's notice. Serve this polenta with Green Bean and Red Pepper Sauté (page 187) for a pleasing match.

2 cups low-fat milk

2 cups water

¼ teaspoon freshly grated nutmeg

½ teaspoon salt

1¼ cups cornmeal

2 tablespoons cold unsalted butter, cut into bits

4 tablespoons grated Parmesan cheese

½ cup grated sharp cheddar cheese

½ cup grated Monterey Jack cheese, *or* Muenster cheese

Serves 4

❶ Generously butter a 9-inch pie plate or shallow 1-quart baking dish and set aside.

❷ Combine the milk, water, nutmeg, and salt in a heavy medium saucepan and bring to a boil. Reduce the heat to a simmer and very slowly sprinkle in the cornmeal, whisking continuously. Cook 5 minutes, or until the cornmeal mixture pulls away from the sides of pan.

❸ Remove the pan from the heat. Whisk in 1½ tablespoons of the butter and 2 tablespoons of the Parmesan cheese.

❹ With a rubber spatula, spread half the polenta mixture in the prepared pie plate or baking dish, then top with the grated cheddar and Monterey Jack cheeses. Spread on the remaining polenta, then sprinkle on the remaining 2 tablespoons Parmesan cheese and dot with the remaining ½ tablespoon of butter.

❺ Let the polenta sit at least 15 minutes, or cover and chill for up to 24 hours. When ready to cook, preheat the oven to 400°F. Bake uncovered 30 minutes, or until golden brown and bubbly.

BARLEY MUSHROOM CASSEROLE

The woodsy flavor of mushrooms permeates this dish and will fill your house with an irresistible aroma. Mashed butternut squash makes a wonderful accompaniment, both in color and texture.

5 tablespoons unsalted butter

2 medium onions, diced

4½ cups (12 ounces) sliced fresh mushrooms

1½ cups barley

¾ teaspoon dried thyme

½ teaspoon salt

Freshly ground black pepper to taste

4½ cups boiling vegetable stock *(see Note, page 133)*

Serves 4

❶ Preheat the oven to 350°F.

❷ Melt the butter in a large skillet over medium-high heat, and add all of the ingredients except the stock. Sauté, stirring frequently, until the mushrooms begin to brown, about 10 minutes.

❸ Scrape the mixture into a deep 2-quart baking dish and pour in the vegetable stock. Cover tightly and bake 60 to 75 minutes, or until all of the liquid is absorbed. (Be careful of the steam when removing the cover.) The barley should have a slightly crunchy texture when done. If it is too hard after all of the stock has been absorbed, add some boiling water and cook 10 to 15 minutes more.

BAKED RICE AND VEGETABLE PILAF WITH CASHEWS

*innamon and cloves
spike this vibrantly colored Indian dish, creating a
wonderfully aromatic blend of flavors. Serve this
with hot, buttered pita bread.*

½ cup raw cashews *(see Note)*

2 tablespoons unsalted butter

1 tablespoon vegetable oil

1 medium onion, finely diced

1 garlic clove, minced

½ teaspoon minced fresh ginger

½ teaspoon turmeric

⅛ teaspoon cayenne pepper

1 cinnamon stick

2 cloves

1 bay leaf

1 cup white basmati rice *or* converted rice

1 pound green beans, cut into 1-inch lengths, *or* 1 10-ounce package frozen cut green beans

1 carrot, very thinly diced

⅓ cup raisins

½ teaspoon salt

1¾ cups boiling water

Serves 3 to 4

❶ Preheat the oven to 400°F. Spread the cashews on a baking sheet and lightly toast, stirring occasionally, until golden and fragrant, about 7 minutes.

❷ Melt the butter with the oil in a large skillet over medium heat. Add the onion, garlic, and ginger, and sauté 2 minutes. Mix in the turmeric, cayenne, cinnamon stick, cloves, and bay leaf and cook 1 minute longer, stirring constantly. Mix in the rice and toss to coat.

❸ Scrape the rice mixture into a 2-quart baking dish. Stir in the green beans, carrot, raisins, cashews, and salt. (You can prepare the dish to this point up to 4 hours in advance, refrigerating it.) Pour in the boiling water and tightly cover the dish.

❹ Bake about 40 minutes, or until all of the liquid is absorbed. (Be careful when you remove the cover; there will be a lot of steam.) Remove the cinnamon stick and bay leaf, fluff with a fork, and let sit, covered, 5 minutes before serving.

☛*Note:* Raw cashews can be purchased at any natural foods store.

RICE, BROCCOLI, AND FETA CHEESE SAUTÉ

The tang of feta cheese gives this simple dish character. For a pleasing accompaniment, try sliced tomatoes drizzled with vinaigrette.

1 cup white or brown rice

2 cups water

½ teaspoon salt

2 teaspoons vegetable oil

¼ cup olive oil

4 garlic cloves, minced

2 medium tomatoes, cored, seeded, and diced

1 bunch broccoli, stalks peeled and cut into bite-size pieces (about 5 cups)

½ teaspoon dried oregano

¼ cup water

1 cup (about 5 ounces) crumbled feta cheese

Freshly ground black pepper

Serves 2 to 3

❶ Combine the rice, water, salt, and oil in a small saucepan and bring to a boil over high heat. Lower the heat to simmer and cook until all of the water is absorbed (20 minutes for white rice and 45 minutes for brown rice). When done, remove from the heat and keep covered.

❷ In a large skillet, heat the olive oil over medium heat. Sauté the garlic 2 minutes, stirring frequently. Do not brown. Add the tomatoes and sauté 2 minutes more. Add the broccoli and oregano, toss well, pour in the water, and cover the pan. Raise the heat to medium-high and cook 5 minutes, or until the broccoli is tender but not mushy. (Remove the cover occasionally and toss the mixture.)

❸ Stir in the hot rice, feta cheese, and black pepper to taste. Serve immediately.

RICE WITH CHICK-PEAS, HERBS, AND SUN-DRIED TOMATOES

A wonderful blending of flavors and textures makes this simple dish special. A steamed vegetable such as broccoli, zucchini, or green beans is all you need for a side dish.

2 tablespoons unsalted butter

1 tablespoon olive oil

2 cups freshly cooked chick-peas (page 161), *or* 1 15-ounce can chick-peas, rinsed and drained

1½ tablespoons chopped, drained sun-dried tomatoes packed in oil *(see Note)*

⅓ cup minced fresh parsley

2½ to 3 cups cold cooked white or brown rice

1 teaspoon minced fresh basil, *or* ¼ teaspoon dried

¼ teaspoon dried oregano

Salt to taste

Freshly ground black pepper to taste

¼ cup grated Parmesan cheese

Serves 3

❶ Heat 1 tablespoon of the butter with the olive oil in a large skillet over medium heat. Add the chick-peas, sun-dried tomatoes, and parsley and cook 3 minutes.

❷ Add the rice, basil, oregano, salt, and pepper and toss well. Sprinkle on 2 tablespoons water. Cook, tossing frequently, until the rice is hot, about 10 minutes.

❸ Cut the remaining 1 tablespoon butter into bits and mix it into the rice. Sprinkle on the Parmesan cheese, toss, and serve.

☛*Note:* If you do not have sun-dried tomatoes on hand, try substituting one seeded and minced fresh medium tomato.

ESSENTIALLY VEGETABLES

Fresh vegetables are such an important part of a healthful diet that they deserve special treatment that enables them to play more than a supporting role.

Many people avoid using fresh vegetables when they need to be quick in the kitchen. I have found a way around this tendency by doing prep work well in advance of cooking. That is, I peel, chop, or slice my vegetables at an earlier time; then, when I'm ready to cook, it's a snap.

A tip about storage: Never wash fresh vegetables before you store them in the refrigerator. The extra moisture encourages decay and cuts down considerably on their storage life. Most vegetables should be kept in a plastic bag with a few holes to allow some air circulation. Potatoes, onions, and garlic should remain at room temperature.

ZUCCHINI, TOMATO, AND SWISS CHEESE PIE

The flavors in this pie are fantastic, so do follow the recipe exactly. The crust is made by sprinkling bread crumbs in a buttered pie plate, keeping preparation quick. It's important to use Swiss cheese because its firmness helps hold the pie together. Serve this pie with Provençal Potatoes (page 179) for a great combination.

1 tablespoon unsalted butter

¼ cup bread crumbs

1½ tablespoons olive oil

1 medium onion, diced

2 garlic cloves, minced

2 medium tomatoes, seeded and diced

3 medium zucchini, quartered lengthwise and thinly sliced

½ teaspoon fennel seed, crushed

¼ teaspoon salt

Freshly ground black pepper to taste

3 large eggs

⅓ cup milk

¼ pound grated or sliced (about 1⅓ cups) Swiss cheese

3 tablespoons grated Parmesan cheese

Serves 4

❶ Preheat the oven to 375°F. Using ½ tablespoon of the butter, grease a pie plate, then sprinkle the bread crumbs over the bottom and sides.

❷ Heat the olive oil in a large skillet over medium heat. Add the onion and garlic and sauté 10 minutes. Stir in the diced tomatoes and sauté 5 minutes. Raise the heat to high. Mix in the zucchini, fennel seed, salt, and pepper. Cook until the zucchini is barely tender, about 5 minutes. (The mixture should begin to stick to the pan.) Remove the pan from the heat and cool 5 minutes. (The recipe may be prepared in advance to this point and chilled up to 24 hours. Bring to room temperature before proceeding.)

❸ Beat the eggs in a large bowl. Stir in the milk, then mix in the zucchini mixture. Pour half into the prepared pie plate, top with the Swiss cheese, then pour on the remaining vegetable mixture. Sprinkle the Parmesan cheese all over the top and dot with the remaining ½ tablespoon of the butter.

❹ Bake 30 minutes, or until a knife inserted in the center comes out clean and the top is golden brown. Let sit 10 minutes before cutting.

MUSHROOM PIE

Savory, juicy mushrooms stand supreme in this pie, which is made with a crumb crust. Try serving it with something colorful but not overpowering, such as Couscous Pilaf with Peas (page 176).

½ tablespoon unsalted butter, softened

⅓ cup bread crumbs

2 tablespoons olive oil

2 garlic cloves, minced

2 medium onions, diced

4 celery ribs, thinly sliced

1½ pounds (about 8 cups) finely chopped (not minced) fresh mushrooms

½ teaspoon dried thyme

½ teaspoon paprika

Dash cayenne pepper

2 tablespoons unbleached flour

¾ cup milk

½ teaspoon salt

2 large eggs, beaten

Serves 4

❶ Preheat the oven to 375°F. Grease a 9-inch pie plate with the butter, sprinkle in the bread crumbs, and rotate the plate until the bottom and sides are coated (there will be a loose layer of crumbs remaining on the bottom).

❷ Heat the olive oil in a large skillet over medium-high heat, then sauté the garlic, onions, and celery 5 minutes.

❸ Raise the heat to high, stir in the mushrooms, thyme, paprika, and cayenne. Cook, stirring often, 10 minutes, or until the juices have almost completely evaporated.

❹ Sprinkle on the flour, stir to coat the mixture, and cook 1 minute. Stir in the milk and salt and cook 1 minute more. Scrape into a large bowl and let cool until just warm.

❺ Stir the beaten eggs into the mushroom mixture and spoon into the prepared pie plate. Bake 30 minutes, or until a knife comes out clean when inserted in the sides of the pie or almost clean when inserted in the center. Let the pie sit on a cooling rack 10 minutes before cutting into wedges.

BROCCOLI CALZONES

A calzone is like a minia-ture pizza folded in half to make a filled turnover. Here broccoli, tomatoes, provolone cheese, and mozzarella are combined to make a delicious stuffing with a slightly smoky flavor.

Frozen pizza dough is a great find for cooks who are seeking shortcuts but want to cook with additive-free ingredients. Most supermarkets carry frozen pizza dough that contains only flour, water, yeast, and salt, so choose this type if available.

1 pound frozen pizza dough, thawed

2 tablespoons olive oil plus additional for dough

4 cups finely chopped broccoli

2 garlic cloves, minced

2 medium tomatoes, cored, seeded, and finely diced

¼ teaspoon dried oregano

¼ teaspoon dried basil

Freshly ground black pepper to taste

6 ounces smoked provolone cheese, cut into 6 slices

6 ounces mozzarella cheese, cut into 6 slices

1 large egg

Makes 6 calzones

❶ While the dough is thawing, heat 2 tablespoons of the olive oil in a large skillet over medium heat. Add the broccoli and sauté 2 minutes, then add 2 tablespoons water and cover the pan. Cook 5 minutes, or until the broccoli is tender.

❷ Remove the cover, stir in the garlic, tomatoes, oregano, basil, and pepper. Raise the heat to high and cook, uncovered, until all the liquid evaporates, about 2 minutes. Scrape into a bowl and let cool to room temperature.

❸ Preheat the oven to 375°F. Divide the pizza dough into 6 pieces of equal size. Roll each piece into a ball, and use a rolling pin to flatten each ball into a 6-inch circle. Brush the top of each round with olive oil to within ½ inch of the edges. With your finger, rub the outer edges of the dough circles with some water to help the calzone seal.

❹ On the bottom half of each round of dough, place 1 slice of provolone, top it with ⅙ of the broccoli filling, and add 1 slice of mozzarella. Fold the dough over to make a half-moon and pinch the edges to seal.

❺ Beat the egg with 1 teaspoon water. Brush the top of each calzone with some of this egg wash. Place the calzones on a baking sheet and cook 25 minutes, or until golden.

Let the calzones sit for 10 minutes before serving. Be careful when you bite into the calzones because the filling is very hot.

CRUSTY POTATOES, TOMATOES, AND ONIONS BAKED WITH OLIVE OIL AND GARLIC

he onions and tomatoes caramelize and create an irresistible crust in this peasant-style casserole. All you need is a salad to round off the meal.

6 medium (about 2 pounds) potatoes, peeled, halved, and very thinly sliced

3 large onions, halved vertically and thinly sliced

4 garlic cloves, minced

1 28-ounce can plum tomatoes, chopped and drained

¼ cup tomato paste

½ cup fruity olive oil

3 tablespoons water

2 teaspoons dried oregano

Salt to taste

Freshly ground black pepper to taste

Serves 4

❶ Preheat the oven to 400°F. In a large bowl, combine the potatoes, onions, garlic, and tomatoes.

❷ In a small bowl, beat together the tomato paste, olive oil, water, oregano, salt, and pepper. Pour over the vegetable mixture and toss to coat well. Spread this mixture in a 12 × 7 × 2-inch baking dish or other 2½-quart ovenproof shallow dish. Cover tightly with aluminum foil and bake 30 minutes. Remove the foil and bake 45 minutes longer, or until the potatoes are tender.

SCALLOPED KALE AND POTATOES

*K*ale, garlic, and pota-
toes are a distinctly harmonious blending of flavors, each enhancing the other. This crusty-coated
casserole is hearty enough to stand as a main
course, yet could also be a delightful side dish if
served with a light entrée.

1 pound fresh kale, *or* 1
10-ounce package frozen
kale, thawed

5 medium-large potatoes,
peeled and very thinly
sliced

2 garlic cloves, minced

1½ cups grated Swiss cheese

6 tablespoons cold unsalted
butter, cut into bits

½ teaspoon salt

Freshly ground black
pepper to taste

1¼ cups milk

*Serves 2 to 3 as a main
course*

❶ If using fresh kale, thoroughly rinse it and shake off the excess water. Pull the leaves from the stems and discard the stems. Stuff the kale into a medium pot and add about ½ cup water. Cook until the kale just wilts, about 7 minutes. Drain and cool the kale. Squeeze out the remaining water with your hands. Roughly chop the kale and set aside. (If using frozen kale, simply squeeze it dry with your hands and set aside.)

❷ Preheat the oven to 425°F. Generously butter a 10 × 10 × 2-inch baking dish or other large shallow baking dish. Spread half the potato slices on the bottom of the dish. Spread on all of the kale, then sprinkle on the garlic and half of the cheese, butter, salt, and pepper. Top with the remaining potato slices, cheese, butter, salt, and pepper.

❸ Carefully pour in the milk and gently shake the dish to distribute. Bake 50 minutes, or until the potatoes are tender and the top is nicely browned.

VEGETABLE CURRY

There are many different versions of vegetable curry, and this one is my favorite. Its richly flavored sauce, made with coconut milk, is particularly good served on rice, with plain yogurt on the side to provide a soothing contrast. Warm pita bread would be the perfect finishing touch.

1½ cups unsweetened dessicated coconut *(see Note)*

2 cups hot water

3 tablespoons unsalted butter

2 medium onions, diced

2 teaspoons minced ginger

4 garlic cloves, minced

1½ teaspoons turmeric

2 teaspoons ground cumin

2 tablespoons ground coriander

⅛ teaspoon cayenne pepper, or more to taste

2 carrots, very thinly sliced

1 small (1½-pound) cauliflower, broken into bite-size flowerets (about 4 cups)

1 cup diced green beans, fresh or frozen

1 cup freshly cooked (page 161) or canned chick-peas, rinsed and drained

½ teaspoon salt

Hot cooked white or brown rice

Serves 4

❶ To make the coconut milk, combine the coconut and hot water in a blender or food processor and blend 2 minutes. Strain the coconut milk in batches through a sieve, pressing out all the liquid from the pulp with the back of a large spoon. Discard the coconut. You should have about 1½ cups coconut milk.

❷ Melt the butter in a large skillet over medium heat. Add the onions, ginger, and garlic and sauté, tossing often, 10 minutes, or until the onions begin to brown.

❸ Sprinkle on the spices and stir to mix thoroughly. Cook this mixture 2 minutes to blend the flavors.

❹ Stir in the coconut milk and bring to a boil. Add the carrots, cauliflower, green beans, chick-peas, and salt, and toss to coat the vegetables with the sauce. Cover the pan and cook 5 minutes. Remove the cover and continue to cook the curry, tossing often, until the vegetables are tender and the sauce has thickened, about 10 minutes more.

❺ Serve with some rice on the side, and drizzle a spoonful of sauce over the rice.

☛*Note:* Unsweetened dessicated coconut can be purchased in health food stores.

☛*Variations:* Try substituting different vegetables

such as zucchini, peas, or even chopped fresh spinach. (Just mound the spinach on top of the cooked curry and cover the pan. In a few minutes it will be wilted, and it can then be mixed into the vegetables and the sauce.)

CHEESY STUFFED POTATOES

This is one of my family's favorite easy meals. Because it is so substantial, I like to serve only a light salad as an accompaniment. Try these potatoes the next time you have a child who is a fussy eater joining you for dinner.

4 large baking potatoes, well scrubbed

1 tablespoon cold unsalted butter, cut into bits

½ cup sour cream

1 cup finely cubed Muenster cheese

½ cup finely cubed cheddar cheese

1 tablespoon minced fresh parsley

Paprika

Serves 4

❶ Prick the potatoes in a few places, place in the oven, and set the temperature at 400°F. Bake 1 hour, or until tender throughout.

❷ Slice the potatoes in half lengthwise and let cool a few minutes. With a spoon, scoop the flesh into a large bowl, leaving ¼ inch of the flesh in the shell. Divide the butter bits and place in the shells.

❸ Mash the potato flesh with a fork, then stir in the sour cream, cheese, and parsley. Spoon back into the shells, then sprinkle paprika on each stuffed potato. Place the potatoes on a baking sheet. Return to the oven and bake 20 minutes, or until hot and bubbly.

POTATO AND ONION FRITTATA

Frittatas are often cooked in skillets on the stovetop, but I have had equally good results baking them in the oven. I have come to prefer this method because it is more relaxed. I like to precede frittatas with a salad, and serve thick slices of toasted Italian or Portuguese bread or bagels alongside.

¼ cup olive oil

2 medium-large potatoes, peeled and cut into ¼-inch cubes

4 medium onions, finely diced

6 large eggs

¼ cup grated Parmesan cheese

¼ teaspoon salt

Freshly ground black pepper to taste

Serves 3 to 4

❶ Heat the oil in a large, preferably cast-iron or nonstick skillet over medium-high heat until hot but not smoking. Fry the potatoes in one layer until golden and tender all over. Remove with a slotted spoon to a plate.

❷ Place the onions in the pan and cook about 15 minutes, tossing frequently, until the onions are very tender. Meanwhile, preheat the oven to 350°F. Butter a 9-inch pie plate and set aside.

❸ In a large bowl, beat the eggs well. Beat in the cheese, salt, and pepper.

❹ When the onions are done, stir them into the egg mixture along with the potatoes. (If you are not ready to cook the frittata, let the onions and potatoes cool before mixing them with the eggs. The mixture can be refrigerated up to 4 hours. Return to room temperature before baking.) Scrape the egg mixture into the pie plate and bake 15 to 25 minutes, or until a knife inserted in the center of the frittata comes out almost clean. Be careful not to overcook the frittata. (The frittata will take longer to cook if the onions and potatoes cool before being mixed with the eggs.) Cut into wedges and serve.

CRUSTY CAULIFLOWER AND RICOTTA CASSEROLE

he pretty pink hue of this savory dish looks lovely with a spinach salad accompaniment. Try mixing the salad with Double Sesame Dressing (page 93).

2 tablespoons olive oil

2 garlic cloves, minced

½ cup finely diced, drained tomatoes

1 medium (2½-pound) cauliflower, cut into small flowerets (about 6 cups)

3 large eggs

1 cup part-skim ricotta cheese

¾ cup milk

¼ cup grated Parmesan cheese

1 tablespoon minced fresh parsley

¼ teaspoon freshly grated nutmeg

Dash cayenne pepper

Freshly ground black pepper to taste

1 cup grated Muenster cheese

¼ cup bread crumbs

Serves 4

❶ Heat the oil in a large skillet over medium heat. Add the garlic and cook 30 seconds. Do not brown. Add the tomatoes and cook 5 minutes, stirring often. Stir in the cauliflower and toss to coat all over with the tomato mixture. Pour in a few tablespoons water and cover the pan. Cook until the cauliflower is tender, about 7 minutes. Take the pan off the heat and let cool to warm or room temperature.

❷ Preheat the oven to 375°F. Butter a $12 \times 7 \times 2$-inch ovenproof dish or other shallow 2½-quart baking dish.

❸ Beat the eggs in a large bowl. Beat in the ricotta, milk, Parmesan cheese, parsley, nutmeg, cayenne, pepper, and Muenster cheese. Stir in the cauliflower mixture. Spread in the prepared dish and sprinkle on the bread crumbs.

❹ Bake 20 minutes, or until hot and bubbly. Do not overcook, or the casserole will dry out.

WILD MUSHROOM TART
IN PUFF PASTRY

*This elegant entrée
would make a sensational centerpiece for a vegetarian Thanksgiving feast. Although the directions
are lengthy, it is not very time-consuming. Couscous Pilaf with Peas (page 176) would be an ideal
side dish.*

2 tablespoons olive oil

4 garlic cloves, minced

1 medium onion, finely
diced

1 medium tomato, seeded
and very finely chopped

12 ounces cultivated
mushrooms, wiped clean
and thinly sliced (about
4½ cups)

4 ounces wild mushrooms
(such as shiitake, cèpes, or
porcini), stems discarded,
wiped clean, and thinly
sliced *(see Note)*

¼ teaspoon dried thyme

A few dashes cayenne
pepper

⅛ teaspoon freshly grated
nutmeg

2 tablespoons dry white
wine

2 large eggs

¼ cup heavy cream

2 tablespoons minced fresh
parsley

¼ teaspoon salt

Freshly ground black
pepper to taste

❶ Heat the oil in a large skillet over medium-high heat. Add the garlic and onion and sauté 5 minutes. Add the tomato and cook 10 minutes, stirring frequently. Stir in all the mushrooms, thyme, cayenne, and nutmeg. Cook, stirring often, until the mushrooms are tender and most of the juices have evaporated, about 7 minutes. Stir in the wine and cook 5 minutes more, or until mostly evaporated.

❷ Scrape the mushroom mixture into a large bowl and let cool to room temperature. Beat 1 of the eggs and stir in, then mix in the cream, parsley, salt, and pepper. (The recipe may be prepared to this point up to 24 hours in advance. Cover and chill if holding more than 2 hours. Bring to room temperature before proceeding with the next step.)

❸ To prepare the puff pastry, thaw at room temperature 20 to 30 minutes. Preheat the oven to 400°F. Gently unfold the pastry on a lightly floured surface. Roll into an 11 × 14-inch rectangle. Cut a 1-inch-wide strip from each side of the rectangle to make 4 strips. Place the rectangle on an ungreased baking sheet. Beat the remaining egg with 1 tablespoon water. Brush the egg wash evenly over the rectangle. Place the strips along the edges of the

1 sheet (about ½ pound) frozen store-bought puff pastry

Serves 4 generously

rectangle to form walls. Trim as necessary. Brush the strips with some egg wash. Prick the bottom of the pastry all over with a fork.

❹ Bake the crust 7 minutes. Remove from the oven and gently prick the bottom of the crust again to deflate it. Let cool. Reduce the oven temperature to 350°F.

❺ Spoon the mushroom mixture into the tart shell. Bake 25 minutes, or until the filling is set. Let cool 5 minutes before cutting.

☞*Note:* 1 ounce dried wild mushrooms can be substituted. Soak in warm water 30 minutes. Rinse clean. Discard the stems and slice the mushroom caps. If you cannot get fresh or dried wild mushrooms, substitute 4 ounces cultivated mushrooms.

ZUCCHINI TOSTADAS

Juicy pieces of tender zucchini and kidney beans are coated with salsa, spread on crispy flour tortillas, and covered with melted cheese. A simple Mexican treat.

3 tablespoons vegetable oil

8 8-inch flour tortillas
(see Note)

¼ cup olive oil

8 cups thinly sliced
zucchini (from about 4
medium-size, quartered
lengthwise)

½ teaspoon dried oregano

2 cups freshly cooked
kidney beans (page 161), *or* 1
15-ounce can kidney beans,
rinsed and drained

1¼ cups salsa (hot, medium,
or mild)

Salt to taste

Freshly ground black
pepper to taste

4 cups (about 12 ounces)
grated extra-sharp cheddar
cheese

Serves 4 generously

❶ Preheat the broiler. With a pastry brush, lightly coat both sides of each tortilla with the oil and place on a baking sheet (this will have to be done in batches). Broil on both sides until lightly golden and crisp. Cool completely. (The tortillas can be prepared up to 2 days in advance and stored in a plastic bag or tin.)

❷ Reduce the oven heat to 450°F. Heat the olive oil in a large skillet over medium-high heat. Add the zucchini and oregano and sauté, tossing frequently, until the zucchini is tender but still slightly crisp, about 7 minutes. Stir in the kidney beans and salsa and toss to blend. Season with salt and pepper, and remove from the heat.

❸ Using 2 baking sheets, place 2 tortillas on each sheet. Spread one eighth of the zucchini mixture on each tortilla. Sprinkle about ½ cup cheese over each tostada.

❹ Bake 5 minutes, or until the cheese melts and begins to bubble. Serve immediately. Repeat with the remaining ingredients.

☛*Note:* Flour tortillas can be found in the dairy section of most supermarkets.

STUFFED POTATOES WITH CHEESE AND SCALLIONS

The creamy filling in this high-protein version of twice-baked potatoes bubbles and oozes with cheese. As with Cheesy Stuffed Potatoes (page 151), this hearty dish needs only a salad to round off the meal.

4 large baking potatoes, well scrubbed

1 tablespoon cold unsalted butter, cut into bits

1 cup cottage cheese

3 tablespoons low-fat milk

⅓ cup grated Parmesan cheese, plus extra for sprinkling

1 cup (about 5 ounces) diced part-skim mozzarella cheese

2 scallions, thinly sliced

Freshly ground black pepper to taste

Serves 4

❶ Cook and prepare the potatoes, following steps 1 and 2 of Cheesy Stuffed Potatoes (page 151).

❷ In a blender or food processor, combine the cottage cheese and milk and blend until very smooth. Turn off the blender and scrape down the sides as necessary. Scrape the cottage cheese into a bowl; stir in the Parmesan, mozzarella, scallions, and pepper.

❸ Mash the potato pulp with a fork. Stir it into the cheese mixture. Spoon the mixture into the potato shells, then sprinkle the tops with some Parmesan cheese. Place the stuffed potatoes on a cookie sheet and bake 20 minutes, or until bubbly and golden brown.

EGGPLANT PARMESAN WITH RICOTTA AND FRESH BASIL

have always disliked the process of breading and frying eggplant slices because it's messy and time-consuming. No alternative method was satisfactory, until I learned a clever trick. I now brush a thin layer of mayonnaise on both sides of each eggplant slice, coat them with bread crumbs, and broil until golden brown. It's very quick and easy, and this step can be done a day in advance.

This version of Eggplant Parmesan contains ricotta and fresh basil, making it both creamy and flavorful.

2 medium eggplants (about 2 pounds total)

⅓ cup mayonnaise

¾ cup bread crumbs

1½ cups tomato sauce

1 garlic clove, pressed

2 tablespoons dry red wine

1 cup part-skim ricotta cheese

½ cup grated Parmesan cheese

½ pound (about 2½ cups) grated mozzarella cheese

2 tablespoons minced fresh basil, *or* 1 teaspoon dried basil

Serves 4 to 6

❶ Peel the eggplant and slice it ½ inch thick. Place the mayonnaise in a dish and the bread crumbs on a plate. With a pastry brush, lightly coat both sides of each eggplant slice with mayonnaise, then dip in the bread crumbs to coat both sides. Place the slices on a baking sheet and broil on both sides until golden brown and tender but not mushy. Place the eggplant on a platter and let cool.

❷ Preheat the oven to 375°F. Combine the tomato sauce, garlic, and red wine in a medium bowl. In a separate bowl, beat together the ricotta and Parmesan cheeses.

❸ Pour half the sauce into a $12 \times 7 \times 2$-inch baking dish or other 2½-quart baking dish. Cover with half the eggplant slices, then spoon on all the ricotta mixture. Sprinkle on half the mozzarella, then top with all the basil. Place the remaining eggplant slices on top, pour on the remaining sauce, then top with the remaining mozzarella cheese.

❹ Cover the baking dish with aluminum foil. (The recipe may be prepared to this point and chilled up to 8 hours in advance. Bring to room temperature before baking.) Bake, covered, 15 minutes; remove the foil and bake 15 minutes more, or until hot and bubbly. Remove from the oven and let sit 10 minutes before serving.

☛*Variation:* Leftover Eggplant Parmesan makes delicious submarine sandwiches. Reheat it in the oven, then place on heated submarine, grinder, or hero rolls.

FULL OF BEANS

Beans are the best nonmeat source of protein. They also are low in fat, high in fiber, and a great source of B vitamins and iron. In addition, the protein in beans has been shown to help lower cholesterol levels in the blood. With all of these benefits, beans have become an indispensable part of the vegetarian diet.

When used in entrées, as they are in this chapter, beans make highly nutritious dishes and need only a salad to complete the meal. As a general rule, if you want to bolster the protein quality of a bean dish, add either grains, seeds, or some form of dairy products to the meal if these aren't already present in the recipe.

With so many health risks attributed to eating meat, beans—once thought of as poor man's food—are rightfully gaining prominence because they offer so much to the health-conscious diet. (To learn how to cook dried beans, see Freshly Cooked Beans on the opposite page.)

FRESHLY COOKED BEANS

Cooking dried beans at home, rather than purchasing canned, cooked beans, is not a quick method for incorporating beans into meals. But with a little forethought, you can cook a large batch of beans and freeze them in small containers to have them on hand when needed. Cooking beans doesn't take much preparation, just the time necessary for them to cook.

There are two ways to prepare beans for cooking. The first is to soak them overnight; the alternative is to boil them for two minutes, then let them soak for one hour. In both cases the beans should be drained and covered with fresh water before cooking.

The following method applies to kidney beans, chickpeas, cannellini, pinto beans, black beans, navy beans, and black-eyed peas. Lentils and split peas do not have to be precooked.

☛ Pick over the beans to remove any stones, twigs, etc.

☛ Rinse the beans in a strainer under cold running water.

☛ Place the beans in a large bowl and fill with cold water to cover by 2 inches. Cover the bowl and soak overnight. Alternatively, place the beans in a large pot and cover with water by 2 inches. Bring to a boil and cook 2 minutes. Cover the pot, remove from the heat, and soak 1 hour.

☛ Thoroughly drain the beans and discard the soaking liquid. Place beans in a large pot. Cover them with plenty of fresh water, and cook at a lively simmer, partly covered, until tender, 1 to 1½ hours, depending on the size of the bean. If you plan to freeze the beans, slightly undercook them because freezing will make them softer. Drain very well and bring to room temperature before refrigerating or freezing. Use in any recipe that calls for cooked beans.

LENTILS WITH BALSAMIC VINEGAR

ere's one of my favor-
ite ways to eat lentils. The vinegar adds a subtle
tang to this dish, and it's an old trick for aiding
digestion. Serve with a steamed vegetable.

1½ cups lentils

½ cup white basmati rice,
or converted white rice

5 cups water

1 bay leaf

½ teaspoon dried thyme

½ teaspoon salt

Freshly ground black
pepper to taste

2 tablespoons fruity olive oil

2 large onions, diced

2 garlic cloves, minced

1 carrot, thinly sliced

1 tablespoon balsamic
vinegar, *or* red wine vinegar

Serves 4 to 6

❶ Pick over the lentils and discard any stones. Rinse in a strainer and place in a heavy saucepan with the rice, water, bay leaf, thyme, salt, and pepper. Cover, bring to a boil, and cook at a lively simmer 20 to 25 minutes, or until tender but not mushy. (The lentils should retain a very slight crunch.)

❷ Meanwhile, heat the olive oil in a medium skillet. Add the onions, garlic, and carrot and cook over medium-low heat 20 minutes, or until the onions are brown and the carrot is tender.

❸ Drain the lentils and rice very well and return to the pot. Discard the bay leaf. Gently stir the carrot mixture into the lentils along with the vinegar and cook 2 minutes to blend the flavors. Serve immediately.

CHILAQUILES

This dish is best described as a Mexican lasagna. Corn tortilla layers alternated with kidney beans, tomatoes, chiles, sour cream, and cheese are baked in a casserole. Very quick and flavorful.

1½ tablespoons olive oil

2 onions, finely diced

2 garlic cloves, minced

1 28-ounce can tomatoes, finely chopped, with their juice

1 16-ounce can kidney beans, rinsed and drained

1 4-ounce can mild green chiles, minced and drained

12 corn tortillas *(see Note)*, cut into 1-inch strips

1 cup sour cream

2½ cups (about 8 ounces) grated Monterey Jack cheese

Serves 4

❶ Preheat the oven to 350°F. Heat the oil in a large skillet over medium-high heat, add the onions and garlic, and sauté 10 minutes, or until the onions are tender.

❷ Stir in the tomatoes and juice, the kidney beans, and chiles. Boil 5 minutes, stirring occasionally, until the juices begin to thicken. Remove from the heat.

❸ Spread half the sauce in a $10 \times 10 \times 2$-inch or $12 \times 7 \times 2$-inch casserole. Top with half the tortilla strips, half the sour cream, and half the cheese. Complete with the remaining tortillas, then the remaining sauce, sour cream, and cheese.

❹ Bake 35 minutes, or until hot and bubbly.

☛*Note:* Corn tortillas usually can be found in the dairy department of most supermarkets.

MEXICAN RED BEANS AND RICE

If you use canned beans or leftover home-cooked beans, this dish is so easy to prepare that it almost seems like cheating.

1½ cups brown rice, *or* converted white rice

3 cups water

1 tablespoon vegetable oil

½ teaspoon salt

BEANS

2 tablespoons olive oil

2 large onions, finely diced

1 tablespoon chili powder

2 15-ounce cans red kidney beans, rinsed and drained, *or* 4 cups freshly cooked kidney beans (page 161)

1 cup salsa (mild, medium, or hot)

¼ cup water

⅔ cup sour cream

Minced fresh parsley, for garnish

Serves 4

❶ Combine the rice, water, oil, and salt in a medium saucepan, cover, and bring to a boil. Reduce to a simmer, and cook the rice, undisturbed, 45 minutes for brown rice or 20 minutes for white rice, or until all the water is absorbed and the rice begins to stick to the pot.

❷ Meanwhile, prepare the beans. Heat the olive oil in a large skillet over medium-high heat. Add the onions and sauté 10 minutes, or until tender. Sprinkle on the chili powder and cook 1 minute. Toss frequently.

❸ Add the beans, salsa, and water, and cook about 5 minutes, or until the mixture is piping hot. To serve, spread some of the hot rice on each serving plate, and top with a mound of the bean mixture. Place a spoonful of sour cream on top of the beans, and garnish with parsley.

VEGETABLE ENCHILADAS

The heavenly tomato-cream mixture that coats these enchiladas is one of my all-time favorite sauces, and here it gives a delicate touch to a hearty, stick-to-your-ribs Mexican dish.

2 tablespoons olive oil

1 medium onion, diced

2 medium zucchini, quartered lengthwise and thinly sliced

1 teaspoon dried oregano

1 4-ounce can chopped green chiles, drained

1½ cups cooked kidney beans, fresh or canned, rinsed and drained

Salt to taste

Freshly ground black pepper to taste

SAUCE

1 28-ounce can tomato puree

½ cup heavy cream

⅓ cup finely chopped cilantro

1 large garlic clove, pressed

¼ teaspoon salt

Freshly ground black pepper to taste

. . . .

8 8-inch flour tortillas

2 cups grated Monterey Jack cheese

Serves 4

❶ Heat the oil in a large skillet over medium-high heat. Add the onion and sauté 5 minutes. Stir in the zucchini and oregano and cook until tender but not mushy, about 7 minutes. Remove the pan from the heat and stir in the chiles, kidney beans, salt, and pepper. Let the mixture cool.

❷ Preheat the oven to 350°F. To make the sauce, combine the tomato puree, heavy cream, cilantro, garlic, salt, and pepper.

❸ To assemble the enchiladas, pour a layer of sauce on the bottom of 2 large casseroles such as a 12 × 7 × 2-inch baking dish (you don't want to crowd the enchiladas). Spoon one eighth of the bean mixture along the center of a tortilla, then sprinkle on 2 tablespoons of the cheese. Roll the enchilada and place seam-side down in a baking dish (don't worry if the tortilla breaks a bit). Repeat with the remaining tortillas.

❹ Spoon the remaining sauce over all of the enchiladas, and sprinkle some of the remaining 1 cup of the cheese on each enchilada. (The enchiladas may be prepared to this point up to 2 hours in advance, refrigerated, and returned to room temperature before baking.)

❺ Bake 25 minutes, or until hot and bubbly. Let sit 5 minutes before serving.

SPICY STIR-FRIED TOFU, PEPPERS, AND MANDARIN ORANGES

Cook about 1½ cups brown rice approximately 1 hour before (or the same amount of white rice for 30 minutes before) you stir-fry the vegetables, and keep warm.

SAUCE

3 tablespoons tamari soy sauce

¼ cup Chinese rice wine

¼ cup syrup from mandarin oranges (see below)

2 teaspoons cornstarch

½ teaspoon sesame oil

1 teaspoon chili oil

. . . .

3 tablespoons peanut oil

1 pound firm tofu, cut into ½-inch cubes and patted dry

2 garlic cloves, minced

2 teaspoons minced ginger

2 green bell peppers, cored and cut into ¾-inch squares

1 red bell pepper, cored and cut into ¾-inch squares

2 tablespoons water

2 11-ounce cans mandarin oranges in light syrup, well drained and ¼ cup syrup reserved

. . . .

Hot cooked rice

Serves 4

❶ Combine all of the sauce ingredients in a cup and set aside. Make sure all of the remaining ingredients are prepared before you begin stir-frying.

❷ Heat a large skillet or wok over high heat. When hot, pour in 2 tablespoons of the peanut oil. When the oil is hot, add the tofu. Stir-fry until golden all over, about 10 minutes. Remove the tofu from the pan and set aside on a platter. Reduce the heat to medium-high.

❸ Pour in the remaining 1 tablespoon of the oil and add the garlic and ginger. Cook 10 seconds, tossing constantly, then add the green and red peppers. Stir-fry 2 minutes, pour in the water, and cover the pan. Cook 5 minutes, occasionally removing the cover to give the mixture a toss. After 5 minutes, remove the cover and stir-fry until most of the liquid has evaporated.

❹ Return the tofu to the pan and stir-fry 1 minute. Give the sauce a stir, then pour it over the mixture and cook 30 seconds. Place some hot cooked rice on each plate and immediately spoon the tofu and vegetables on the rice. Put equal amounts of mandarin oranges on top of each serving, and let each person gently mix them in.

TOFU. In Japan it's called tofu; in China, dow foo. In both cases, it's bean curd. This increasingly popular food is made by cooking, mashing, and draining soy beans, then mixing nigari, a mineral derived from sea salt, or another coagulant with the drained soy milk (whey) to form curds. The curds are then pressed into cakes to form tofu.

Tofu is an excellent source of protein, a good source of calcium (provided by the coagulant), and low in fat. Because of its mild flavor, it is especially good when prepared in a highly seasoned dish, for it will absorb the flavors around it. A very simple preparation that many people, from toddlers to adults, like is to cut firm tofu into small cubes, pat them dry with a paper towel, and lightly coat with soy sauce.

Tofu is now sold in most supermarkets in the produce section. It is preferable to purchase it in sealed and dated airtight containers rather than in open tubs (as it is sold in most oriental markets), which make it vulnerable to harmful bacteria. Three textures are usually available: extra-firm, firm, and soft. The firm varieties are best for stir-frying and sautéing because they hold together well and won't crumble; the soft variety is suitable for pureeing or creaming in recipes such as salad dressings, dips, and cheese cakes. To simplify matters, I keep firm tofu on hand and use it for all types of preparations because it is very versatile.

If only part of a container of tofu will be used, or if you purchase the tofu in an open tub, you must store the unsealed tofu in a covered dish of water and change the water daily. Spoiled tofu smells sour and has a slimy feel and yellowish cast.

TOFU PROVENÇAL

Try this low-fat dish
served with Bulghur Mushroom Pilaf (page 177).

3 tablespoons olive oil

1 pound firm tofu, cut into ½-inch cubes and patted very dry

3 garlic cloves, minced

2 medium onions, diced

3 cups (almost 1 35-ounce can) plum tomatoes, coarsely chopped with their juice

1 tablespoon tomato paste

2 cups diced green beans

½ teaspoon dried basil

½ teaspoon dried oregano

1 bay leaf

Salt to taste

Freshly ground black pepper to taste

Serves 4

❶ Heat the oil in a large skillet over high heat until hot but not smoking. Add the tofu and stir-fry until golden all over. Remove to a platter and lower the heat to medium.

❷ If the pan is dry, pour in a little more oil. Add the garlic and onions and sauté 5 minutes. Pour the tomatoes and their juice into the onion and garlic mixture, along with the tomato paste, stirring until blended.

❸ Return the tofu to the skillet, toss, and add the green beans, basil, oregano, bay leaf, salt, and pepper. Toss thoroughly, reduce the heat to simmer, and cover the pan. Cook 15 minutes, or until the green beans are tender. If at this point the sauce is too thin, cook uncovered a few minutes, or until it boils down and thickens somewhat. Remove the bay leaf before serving.

TOFU *HOISIN* WITH CASHEWS AND VEGETABLES

*T*o keep this a relaxed meal, completely cook 1½ cups brown or white rice before you begin stir-frying, then keep the rice warm on the back burner or in the oven while you prepare the dish.

4 tablespoons peanut oil

1 pound firm tofu, cut into ½-inch cubes and patted very dry

5 carrots, thinly sliced on the diagonal

3 tablespoons water

½ pound snow peas, tips and strings removed

¾ cup (about 4 ounces) roasted *(see Note)* cashews

1 teaspoon minced fresh ginger

SAUCE

⅓ cup *hoisin* sauce

2 tablespoons tamari soy sauce

2 tablespoons Chinese rice wine, *or* dry sherry

1 tablespoon oriental sesame oil

. . . .

Hot cooked rice

Serves 4

❶ Place all of the ingredients in front of you before you begin stir-frying. Mix the sauce ingredients together in a small cup and keep nearby. Heat 2 tablespoons of the peanut oil in a wok or large skillet over high heat until hot but not smoking. Add the tofu and stir-fry until evenly golden, about 10 minutes. Remove the tofu to a platter and keep it near the stove; reduce the heat to medium high.

❷ Put the carrots in the pan or wok, toss, then pour in the 3 tablespoons water. Immediately cover the pan and cook 3 minutes. Remove the cover. (The water should have evaporated; if not, cook uncovered for a few seconds.) Push the carrots to the sides of the pan to make a well, then pour the remaining 2 tablespoons of the peanut oil into the center of the pan. Let it heat for a few seconds, then toss it onto the carrots.

❸ Add the snow peas, cashews, and ginger and stir-fry 2 minutes. Return the tofu to the pan and stir-fry 1 minute more.

❹ Give the sauce mixture a quick stir and pour it over the tofu and vegetables. Toss to coat and immediately spoon the vegetables onto a platter or into a serving bowl. Serve over rice.

(continued)

☞*Note:* If the roasted cashews are salted, rinse with water in a strainer and pat dry. You can substitute raw cashews from the health food store, but toast them in a 350°F. oven until golden, about 7 minutes, before beginning to cook.

HOISIN SAUCE. Hoisin sauce is a delicious, sweetened soybean-based sauce that also contains garlic and chiles. Avoid brands that include red and yellow dyes and other additives. I often use the China Bowl brand found in many supermarkets and specialty food shops.

SPICY RAGOUT OF VEGETABLES AND TOFU

*T*he traditional French
method of gently cooking a mélange of vegetables
(with tofu instead of meat, in this case) in a small
amount of seasoned liquid makes this ragout a
very tasty, low-fat entree. Serve this alongside hot
brown rice that has been drizzled with olive oil
and sprinkled with Parmesan cheese.

4 tablespoons olive oil

1 pound firm tofu, cut into
½-inch cubes and patted
very dry

6 garlic cloves, minced

¼ teaspoon crushed red
pepper flakes

1 28-ounce can plum
tomatoes, roughly chopped,
with their juice

1 tablespoon minced fresh
basil, *or* ½ teaspoon dried
basil

Salt to taste

Freshly ground black
pepper to taste

1 medium head cauliflower,
cut into bite-size flowerets
(about 5 cups)

2 cups frozen peas, thawed

Serves 4

❶ In a 6-quart pot, heat 3 tablespoons olive oil over medium-high heat. Fry the tofu until golden all over and remove to a platter.

❷ Pour in the remaining 1 tablespoon of the oil, reduce the heat to medium, and sauté the garlic and red pepper flakes until the garlic just begins to get golden, about 2 minutes. Immediately add the chopped tomatoes and their juice, the basil, salt, and pepper and bring to a boil. Cook 3 minutes, then add the cauliflower. Tossing occasionally, cook until the cauliflower is tender but not mushy, about 15 minutes.

❸ Return the tofu to the pot, and stir in the peas. Cook just until both are heated through, about 3 minutes.

SKILLET TOFU, YELLOW SQUASH, AND PEPPERS WITH MELTED CHEESE

his colorful stir-fry has just a hint of tomato sauce that clings to the vegetables with the creamy melted cheese. Serve with rice, Bulghur Mushroom Pilaf (page 177), or buttered egg noodles.

3 tablespoons vegetable oil

1 pound firm tofu, cut into ½-inch cubes and patted very dry

2 medium onions, diced

2 yellow squash, halved lengthwise and thinly sliced

1 green bell pepper, seeded and cubed

½ cup tomato sauce

Freshly ground black pepper to taste

1 cup (about 4 ounces) grated Muenster cheese

Serves 4

❶ Heat the oil in a large skillet over medium-high heat until hot but not smoking. Stir-fry the tofu until golden, about 10 minutes. Remove from the pan with a slotted spoon and set aside on a platter.

❷ If the pan has no oil left, add a little more, and sauté the onions, squash, and pepper until crisp-tender, about 10 minutes.

❸ Return the tofu to the pan, toss, and stir in the tomato sauce. Season with pepper and cook 2 minutes, or until hot and bubbly.

❹ Sprinkle on the cheese, and cover the pan. Cook 1 to 2 minutes, or until the cheese has melted. Serve immediately.

SIDE DISHES

The side dish recipes in this chapter will assist you in menu planning when you lack a certain something to accompany your main course. Or, as I often like to do, you can make a meal of a combination of dishes, such as a tasty prepared vegetable accompanied by buttered egg noodles or brown rice, or select a pilaf or potato recipe and serve it with steamed vegetables.

At the height of summer, when a plentiful supply of all sorts of vegetables is available, turn to this chapter to discover new ways of preparing them.

COUSCOUS PILAF
WITH PEAS

*resh dill enlivens this
light pilaf and gives it a distinctive flavor.*

1 tablespoon olive oil

1 medium onion, finely diced

1 garlic clove, minced

1 cup couscous

1 cup frozen peas, thawed

1 tablespoon minced fresh dill, *or* 1 teaspoon dried

¼ teaspoon salt

Freshly ground black pepper to taste

1½ cups vegetable stock *(see Note)*

1 tablespoon cold unsalted butter, cut into bits

Serves 4

❶ Heat the oil in a medium saucepan over medium heat. Sauté the onion and garlic, stirring often, until very tender, about 10 minutes.

❷ Stir in the couscous, peas, dill, salt, pepper, and vegetable stock. Cover, bring to a boil, and remove from the heat. Let sit until all of the water is absorbed, about 5 minutes. Fluff with a fork, then stir in the butter bits. Serve immediately, or cover again and let sit up to 10 minutes more.

☞*Note:* Vegetable stock can be made with powdered vegetable stock base, available at health food stores.

BULGHUR MUSHROOM PILAF

Golden, medium-textured bulghur, as opposed to the dark, coarse-grain variety, is especially good in this pilaf. Its buttery flavor is enhanced by the mushrooms and scallions.

1 tablespoon unsalted butter

1½ cups (about 4 ounces) finely chopped mushrooms

1 carrot, minced

1 cup golden bulghur

¼ teaspoon dried thyme

¼ teaspoon salt

Freshly ground black pepper to taste

2 cups vegetable stock (*see Note*, page 176)

2 scallions, very thinly sliced

Serves 4

❶ Over medium-high heat, melt the butter in a heavy, medium saucepan. Add the mushrooms and cook, stirring often, 10 minutes. The juices that accumulate will enhance the vegetable stock.

❷ Stir in the carrot, bulghur, thyme, salt, pepper, and vegetable stock. Cover the pan, reduce the heat to a simmer, and cook, undisturbed, 20 minutes, or until all of the liquid has been absorbed.

❸ Remove the pan from the heat, sprinkle on the scallions, and fluff the mixture with a fork. Cover the pan again and let sit 10 minutes. Serve hot as a side dish with a steamed vegetable.

GREEN BEAN SALAD WITH LEMON, DILL, AND FETA CHEESE

This tasty treatment of green beans works well with delicate summer beans as well as mature green beans.

1 pound green beans, tips removed

3 tablespoons olive oil

2 tablespoons fresh lemon juice

Freshly ground black pepper to taste

2 tablespoons minced fresh dill, *or* 1 teaspoon dried dill weed

3 tablespoons slivered red onion

¼ cup crumbled feta cheese

Salt

Serves 4

❶ Steam the green beans until crisp-tender. Rinse under cold running water until cold throughout. Drain very well, and pat dry with a paper or cotton towel.

❷ Combine the olive oil, lemon juice, and pepper in a serving bowl. Stir in the green beans and toss. Sprinkle on the dill and onion and toss again. Let sit 30 minutes, or cover and chill for up to 4 hours. Serve at room temperature. Just before serving, sprinkle on the feta cheese and toss again. Taste for salt.

PROVENÇAL POTATOES

If I had to choose one potato dish from among them all, it would be Provençal potatoes.

4 medium (about 1 pound) red-skinned boiling potatoes

3 tablespoons olive oil

2 garlic cloves, finely chopped

1 scallion, very thinly sliced

Salt to taste

Freshly ground black pepper to taste

Serves 2 to 3

❶ Peel the potatoes and slice them in half lengthwise. Slice each half into ¼-inch-thick half-moons.

❷ Heat the olive oil in a large, heavy skillet over medium-high heat. Add the potatoes and cook, tossing frequently, about 15 minutes, or until tender and evenly browned.

❸ Reduce the heat to medium, then sprinkle on the garlic and scallion. Cook, tossing constantly, about 2 minutes more, or until the scallions are hot and tender. Season with salt and pepper and serve immediately.

☛*Note:* If you want to double this recipe, use two large skillets to avoid overcrowding.

SWEET POTATOES ANNA

This treatment of sweet potatoes makes a crusty "pie." Cut it into wedges and serve it alongside steamed vegetables for a simple, delicious meal.

6 tablespoons unsalted butter, melted

2 pounds (about 4 medium) sweet potatoes or yams

4 tablespoons grated Parmesan cheese

¼ teaspoon freshly ground nutmeg

Salt

Freshly ground black pepper to taste

Serves 4

❶ Preheat the oven to 425°F. Pour 1 tablespoon of the melted butter in an 8-inch round cake pan and brush it all over the bottom and sides with a pastry brush.

❷ Peel the potatoes and cut them into paper-thin slices. Layer one-quarter of the potato slices in concentric circles in the prepared pan, then dab on one-quarter of the melted butter with the pastry brush. Mix the cheese with the nutmeg. Sprinkle on one-quarter of the cheese mixture and season lightly with salt and pepper. Repeat 3 times, ending with the cheese mixture. The potatoes will have risen above the pan slightly; push them down with your hand to flatten. Cover the pan with foil. (The recipe to this point may be prepared up to 24 hours in advance and refrigerated. Return to room temperature before baking.)

❸ Bake 45 minutes, then uncover and bake 30 to 40 minutes longer, or until tender. Let sit 5 minutes. Drain off any excess butter.

❹ Run a knife around the edges of the potatoes and invert onto a platter. Cut into wedges to serve.

SCALLOPED SWEET POTATOES

I prefer to use yams — bright-orange sweet potatoes — for their attractive color. Serve this at your next Thanksgiving feast as a welcome change from traditional sugary sweet potato dishes.

6 medium-large (about 2½–3 pounds) sweet potatoes or yams

4 tablespoons cold unsalted butter, cut into bits

1½ cups grated sharp cheddar cheese

Salt to taste

Freshly ground black pepper to taste

1¼ cups low-fat milk

Serves 4 to 6

❶ Preheat the oven to 425°F. Lightly butter a 10 × 10 × 2-inch or other large, shallow baking dish. Peel the sweet potatoes and cut them in half lengthwise, then slice them into paper-thin half-moons.

❷ Spread half the sliced potatoes in the bottom of the baking dish. Sprinkle with half the butter bits and grated cheese, and season with salt and pepper. Spread the remaining sweet potato slices on top, then the remaining butter and grated cheese.

❸ Slowly pour the milk into the corner of the dish, then gently shake the dish to distribute the milk. Cook, uncovered, 45 minutes, or until the potatoes are tender when pierced with a knife. Let sit 10 minutes before serving.

YELLOW SQUASH
AU GRATIN

This buttery gratin with an overtone of onion has become my favorite way to serve yellow squash.

2 pounds (about 4 medium) yellow summer squash, thinly sliced

1 medium onion, minced

⅓ cup sour cream

1 large egg, beaten

4 tablespoons butter, melted

2 teaspoons sugar

½ teaspoon salt

⅓ cup bread crumbs

Serves 4 to 6

❶ Steam the squash until very tender. Mash it in a large bowl until almost smooth. Drain out any liquid.

❷ Preheat the oven to 375°F. Mix the onion, sour cream, egg, 2 tablespoons of the melted butter, sugar, and salt into the mashed squash.

❸ Scrape the mixture into a medium gratin dish or an 8-inch square baking dish. Sprinkle the bread crumbs on top and drizzle on the remaining melted butter. Bake 45 minutes. Let sit 10 minutes before serving.

BRAISED FENNEL

*ry this aromatic dish
with some hot buttered rice and crusty French
bread for a simple meal.*

2 medium fennel bulbs,
with tops

3 tablespoons olive oil

3 large shallots, finely diced

1 14-ounce can plum
tomatoes, finely chopped,
with their juice

3 tablespoons water

Salt to taste

Freshly ground black
pepper to taste

2 tablespoons grated
Parmesan cheese

Serves 4

❶ Wash the fennel and pat very dry. Remove about 1 cup of the feathery tops and set aside. Cut the stalks from the fennel bulbs. Remove the 2 tough outer leaves from each bulb and discard. Cut each bulb into quarters vertically, making sure to keep the core intact on each piece.

❷ Heat the olive oil in a flameproof baking dish over medium heat. When hot, sauté the fennel quarters 10 minutes, turning them frequently. They should begin to brown.

❸ Add the shallots and toss to mix. Cook 10 minutes more.

❹ Roughly chop the reserved tops and add to the pan. Stir in the chopped tomatoes and their juice, the water, salt, and pepper.

❺ Cover the dish and reduce the heat to simmer. Cook 30 minutes, or until the bulbs are tender when pierced with a knife. Turn the fennel occasionally while it cooks. At this point, the sauce should be nice and thick; if it is watery, boil uncovered until it thickens.

❻ Sprinkle the Parmesan cheese on each fennel quarter. For a nice brown crust, put the dish under the broiler for 1 to 2 minutes, or until golden brown.

GRATED ZUCCHINI SAUTÉ

Grated zucchini with the juices squeezed out can be sautéed very quickly and keep its crunchy texture.

3 medium zucchini

1 tablespoon olive oil

1 tablespoon minced fresh basil, *or* ½ teaspoon dried

Salt to taste

Freshly ground black pepper to taste

2 teaspoons cold unsalted butter, cut into bits

1 tablespoon grated Parmesan cheese

Serves 4

❶ Cut the ends from the zucchini and discard. Shred the zucchini using a hand grater. Place the zucchini in a cotton kitchen towel and gather it into a ball. Twist hard to remove all the juices. Scrape the grated zucchini into a bowl.

❷ Heat the oil in a large skillet over medium-high heat. Add the zucchini, basil, salt, and pepper and sauté, tossing often, until crisp-tender, about 5 minutes. Sprinkle on the butter and Parmesan cheese, toss, and serve.

TOMATOES PROVENÇAL

Tomatoes are halved and topped with bread crumbs spiked with garlic and herbs, then drizzled with olive oil and baked until juicy.

2 large firm ripe tomatoes

2 slices white bread

2 garlic cloves, minced

1 tablespoon minced fresh basil, *or* 1 teaspoon dried basil

2 tablespoons minced fresh parsley

2 teaspoons minced fresh chives

Salt to taste

Freshly ground black pepper to taste

6 tablespoons olive oil

Serves 2 to 4

❶ Preheat the oven to 375°F. With a small pointed knife, core each tomato, cutting only as deep as necessary. Cut each tomato in half horizontally and gently squeeze each half to remove the seeds and juice. Use your fingertip to help push out the seeds.

❷ Lightly toast the bread. Tear it into pieces and process in a blender or food processor to make crumbs. In a small bowl, combine the crumbs, garlic, basil, parsley, chives, salt, and pepper. Moisten with 4 tablespoons of the olive oil to make the mixture sticky.

❸ Fill each tomato half with the crumb mixture, pushing it into the cavities and mounding it on top. Place the stuffed tomatoes in a lightly oiled shallow baking dish. Drizzle the remaining 2 tablespoons of the olive oil over the tomatoes. Bake 20 to 30 minutes, or until the stuffing is golden on top and the tomatoes are juicy.

OVEN FRIES

Here's an easy, low-fat method for making French fries (see Note). Cut potatoes are tossed in a little oil, then placed on a baking sheet and cooked in a hot oven to produce crisp, tender fries.

3 medium baking potatoes
1 tablespoon vegetable oil
Salt

Serves 2 to 4

❶ Leaving the skins on, scrub the potatoes thoroughly and pat dry. Cut each potato lengthwise into 16 wedges about ¼ inch thick. Place the potatoes in a large bowl, cover with cold water, and soak 30 minutes. Meanwhile, preheat the oven to 475°F.

❷ Thoroughly drain the potatoes and pat very dry with a cotton or paper towel. Return to the bowl. Pour on the oil and toss to coat evenly.

❸ Lightly oil a baking sheet. Spread the potatoes in one layer. Bake 15 minutes. Turn the potatoes over and bake 10 to 15 minutes more, or until golden and tender. Season with salt and serve immediately.

☞*Note:* You can also make home fries using this low-fat method. Peel waxy boiling potatoes and cut them into pieces the size of a half-dollar. Toss with oil (olive oil is delicious), and bake as directed. (Chopped onion and a generous sprinkling of chili powder mixed with the potato slices before baking add a spunky flavor.)

GREEN BEAN AND RED
PEPPER SAUTÉ

¾ pound green beans

¼ cup water

1 large red bell pepper,
cored and cut into ½-inch-
wide strips

1 tablespoon olive oil

1 garlic clove, pressed

½ tablespoon unsalted
butter

Serves 4

❶ Snap the ends of the green beans and discard.
Leave the beans whole and place in a large skillet.
Pour in the water, cover the pan, and bring to a boil
over medium-high heat. Cook 5 to 7 minutes, or
until almost tender. Drain out all the water.

❷ Lower the heat to medium. Stir in the red pepper,
olive oil, and garlic. Sauté 2 minutes, stirring frequently. Cover the pan and cook 3 minutes more, or
until the red peppers are crisp but tender. Stir in
the butter and serve immediately.

THE
VEGETARIAN
BARBECUE

Vegetarians finally can be included in snazzy outdoor cookouts with dishes that transcend the old standbys of corn-on-the-cob and potato salad. Grilled vegetables are a splendid contribution to barbecues, freeing the imaginations of meat-eaters and vegetarians alike.

One of the great appeals of cooking on the grill is its ease, and the simplistic approach works well with vegetables. Marinades requiring little or no cooking saturate vegetables, tofu, and tempeh, the main components of the vegetarian barbecue, to make satisfying main courses. The smoky flavor produced by the hot coals enhances these ingredients in a special way, unlike any indoor cooking method.

LEMON-SOY MARINADE

ere is a tasty marinade for grilling — one that will have you shamelessly licking your fingers.

½ cup peanut oil *or* vegetable oil

3 tablespoons fresh lemon juice

4½ tablespoons tamari soy sauce

2½ tablespoons oriental sesame oil

1 scallion, very thinly sliced

3 garlic cloves, pressed

1½ teaspoons ground ginger

Makes about 1¼ cups

❶ Combine all the ingredients in a jar with a screw-on top and shake vigorously. Use for Tofu Shish Kebab (page 193), Grilled Mushrooms (below), and Grilled Eggplant Slices (page 198).

GRILLED MUSHROOMS

hese mouth-watering mushrooms are so delectable you can serve a whole skewer to each person as a side dish.

1 recipe Lemon-Soy Marinade (above)

1½ pounds mushrooms, rinsed and patted dry

1 teaspoon minced fresh parsley

Serves 4

❶ Prepare the marinade and pour into a large bowl. Stir in the mushrooms and toss to coat well. Let sit 4 to 6 hours, tossing occasionally.

❷ Thread the mushrooms on skewers, running the skewers through the stems and out the caps.

❸ Grill over hot coals 15 minutes, turning every 5 minutes or so. Brush with some of the leftover marinade while cooking. Brush with marinade and sprinkle the minced parsley over the mushrooms just before serving.

TOFU SHISH KEBAB WITH LEMON-SOY MARINADE

1 recipe Lemon-Soy
Marinade (page 192)

1 pound extra-firm or firm
tofu, cut into ¾-inch cubes
and patted very dry

16 cherry tomatoes

1 large green bell pepper,
cored and cut into 1-inch
squares

½ large red onion, cut
vertically into thirds and
chunks separated

12 fresh mushrooms, rinsed
and patted dry

Serves 4

❶ Prepare the marinade. Place the tofu in a medium bowl, pour on ⅓ of the marinade, and toss gently to coat. Cover and refrigerate 4 to 8 hours.

❷ In a large bowl, combine the tomatoes, pepper, onions, and mushrooms. Pour on the remaining marinade and toss well. Let sit for 4 to 8 hours. (Cover and refrigerate if making longer than 4 hours in advance.)

❸ Alternately thread the tofu and vegetables on skewers. Cook over hot coals about 15 minutes, turning the skewers every 5 minutes. Brush with some of the leftover marinade a few times while cooking, and again just before serving.

TEMPEH TERIYAKI SHISH KEBAB

This sweet and spicy sauce is great for barbecuing; it coats well and superbly enhances the charcoal flavor.

MARINADE

¼ cup peanut oil *or* vegetable oil

¼ cup tamari soy sauce

¼ cup sherry

2 garlic cloves, pressed

1 teaspoon ground ginger

2 tablespoons molasses

. . . .

10 ounces tempeh, cut into 1-inch cubes

1 red bell pepper, cored and cut into 1-inch squares

1 small yellow squash, quartered lengthwise and cut into 1-inch chunks

½ large red onion, cut vertically into thirds and chunks separated

Serves 4

❶ In a large bowl, combine the ingredients for the marinade and whisk together until blended. (The marinade can be made up to 24 hours in advance and refrigerated.)

❷ Stir in the tempeh, red pepper, squash, and red onion. Let sit 4 to 8 hours. (If holding longer than 4 hours, cover and refrigerate.) Stir occasionally to coat everything well.

❸ Alternately thread the tempeh and vegetables on skewers. Cook on a hot grill 15 minutes, turning the skewers every 5 minutes. Occasionally brush some of the leftover marinade on the skewers while cooking, and again just before serving.

GRILLED EGGPLANT WITH SPICY PEANUT SAUCE

his spicy Indonesian sauce is the perfect foil for the mild taste of eggplant. For a colorful accompaniment, serve this with Smoked Vegetables with Cumin Dressing (page 196).

2 teaspoons oriental sesame oil

2 garlic cloves, minced

⅛ teaspoon crushed red pepper flakes

⅓ cup crunchy natural-style peanut butter

2 teaspoons tamari soy sauce

2 teaspoons fresh lime juice

1½ teaspoons sugar

⅓ cup water

. . . .

2 medium eggplants

Vegetable oil for brushing

Serves 4

❶ In a small saucepan, heat the sesame oil over medium heat. Add the garlic and red pepper and cook 30 seconds.

❷ With a whisk or fork, beat in the peanut butter, soy sauce, lime juice, sugar, and water. The sauce should be the consistency of hot fudge sauce. Add a few drops water if necessary. Keep barely warm while cooking the eggplant. (You can make this sauce in advance and chill it for up to 24 hours. Warm over low heat.)

❸ Slice the eggplant ½ inch thick. Brush both sides of each slice with oil, then grill on a rack over hot coals 7 to 10 minutes, turning once. The eggplant should be tender, not mushy. (I like to grill with the cover closed for extra-smoky flavor.) Serve with a spoonful of warm peanut sauce on each slice.

SMOKED VEGETABLES
WITH CUMIN DRESSING

*S*erve this delicious con-
coction at your next barbecue, and it will be a
glowing success (pun intended!). A colorful assortment of vegetables grilled with the cover closed
acquire a deep, smoky flavor. If you have more
dishes to grill, prepare this first; it can sit for a
few hours.

DRESSING

½ teaspoon cumin seeds

2 garlic cloves, minced

2 tablespoons fresh lemon
juice

1 teaspoon tamari soy sauce

⅓ cup olive oil

Salt to taste

Freshly ground black
pepper to taste

VEGETABLES

1 medium yellow squash,
cut lengthwise ½ inch thick

1 medium zucchini, cut
lengthwise ½ inch thick

1 medium onion, cut into
¾-inch-thick slices

1 large red bell pepper

Serves 4

❶ To make the dressing, toast the cumin seeds in a small skillet over medium heat. Shake the pan a few times to prevent burning. Pour the seeds into a small bowl and let cool. Crush them a bit with a mortar and pestle, or roll with a rolling pin. Return them to the bowl. Whisk in the remaining dressing ingredients.

❷ Brush the yellow squash, zucchini, and onion slices on both sides with some of the dressing. Place on a grill over hot coals, along with the whole bell pepper. Close the cover and cook about 10 minutes, turning the vegetables after 5 minutes. (The bell pepper should be turned frequently to char it evenly. It will cook 15 to 20 minutes.) When done, the vegetables should be tender but still crunchy.

❸ Place the vegetables on a platter and let cool. When the bell pepper is done, place it in a paper or plastic bag, close tightly, and steam for 10 minutes. Cut the yellow squash, zucchini, and onion into large chunks and stir them into the remaining dressing. Peel the bell pepper under cold running water, core it, and pat dry. Cut the pepper into large chunks and stir it into the vegetable mixture. Serve warm or at room temperature.

GARLICKY GRILLED TOMATOES

These tomatoes are extra-juicy and flavorful, and are a wonderful addition to a meal cooked on the grill.

2 large firm ripe tomatoes

1 garlic clove, pressed

1 teaspoon minced fresh basil, *or* ¼ teaspoon dried basil

Salt to taste

Freshly ground black pepper to taste

2 tablespoons olive oil

Serves 2 to 4

❶ With a very shallow cut, remove the cores from the tomatoes. Cut each tomato in half horizontally, then gently squeeze out the juice and seeds.

❷ Place 2 tomato halves on each of 2 double sheets of aluminum foil large enough to enclose them. Sprinkle the garlic, basil, salt, and pepper over each tomato. Drizzle on the olive oil. Fold the foil over the tomatoes to form well-sealed packets.

❸ Place the packets on a hot grill and cook about 15 minutes. Check one of the packets; when done, the tomatoes will be juicy and tender but not mushy. Serve with the accumulated juices poured over them.

GRILLED EGGPLANT SLICES

The eggplant slices soak up the Lemon-Soy Marinade and become nice and juicy.

1 medium eggplant

1 recipe Lemon-Soy Marinade (page 192)

Serves 4

❶ Keeping the skin on, slice the eggplant ½ inch thick.

❷ Prepare the Lemon-Soy Marinade and pour into a large bowl.

❸ One by one, dip the eggplant slices in the marinade, then place on a hot grill. Cook 15 minutes, turning the eggplant after 7 minutes. Brush the slices with marinade throughout the cooking time, and again just before serving.

GRILLED CORN-ON-THE-COB

This ultrasimple method produces very tender, tasty corn. Simplicity at its best.

Fresh sweet corn

Butter

Salt

❶ Soak the desired amount of corn in the husk in a sink or tub full of cold water for 15 minutes.

❷ Remove the corn from the water, shake off the excess, and place on the grill over hot coals. Cover the grill and cook 30 minutes, rotating the corn one-third of a turn every 10 minutes. The husks will blacken, but the corn inside will not burn.

❸ Let cool a few minutes, or until easy to handle. Peel off the husks and the silk (the silk should come off easily in clumps). Serve immediately with butter and salt.

CORN-ON-THE-COB WITH CHILI-GARLIC BUTTER

The cornhusks are pulled back halfway to slather on a flavored butter, then closed to let the corn steam. A delicious method of grilling corn.

3 tablespoons unsalted butter, softened

1 garlic clove, pressed

1 teaspoon chili powder

6 ears fresh sweet corn

Makes 6 ears of corn

❶ Thoroughly combine the butter, garlic, and chili powder in a small bowl. Set aside.

❷ Soak the corn in the husk in a sink or tub filled with cold water 15 minutes. Remove the corn from the water, shake off the excess, and pull the husks back halfway. Remove as much silk as you can. Rub the flavored butter all over the exposed corn. Pull the husks back over the corn and twist shut. Tightly wrap each ear of corn in foil.

❸ Immediately place the corn on the grill over hot coals (don't delay, or the wet husks will dry out). Close the cover and cook 35 minutes, rotating each ear one-third of a turn every 10 minutes.

❹ Remove the foil from each ear. Cool a few minutes until easy to handle, then remove the husks. Serve immediately.

DESSERTS

Dessert, for me, is not an everyday affair but an occasional treat that I relish without guilt. I avoid sweets on a regular basis and allow myself a pleasurable concoction from time to time.

When planning menus, the choice of a dessert should always depend on how rich the other courses are. Not only will the dessert taste better if it is in balance with the rest of the meal, but your guests will feel better as well. If you choose to serve a pasta dish with a cream-based sauce, then a light dessert such as Strawberry and Peach Compote (page 225) will be refreshing and satisfying. On the other hand, if your dinner includes a light entrée such as Bulghur Salad with Corn, Zucchini, and Shredded Basil (page 80), then a seductive dessert such as Toasted Almond Mocha Ice Cream Torte (page 204) would be very welcome.

Sensible eating allows you to splurge occasionally, and you'll be none the worse for such indulgences.

ICE CREAM TRUFFLE PIE WITH RASPBERRY SAUCE

I *can easily say that this is one of the best desserts I've ever tasted. A dense chocolate truffle layer sandwiched between vanilla and chocolate ice cream gives this pie a captivating texture, while the tartness of the raspberry sauce beautifully offsets its sweetness.*

⅔ cup chocolate wafer crumbs (about 14 wafers; *see Note,* page 206)

3 tablespoons unsalted butter, melted

1 pint chocolate ice cream

1 cup (6 ounces) semisweet chocolate chips

⅓ cup heavy cream

1 pint vanilla ice cream

2 tablespoons finely chopped walnuts

1 10-ounce package frozen raspberries in syrup, thawed

1 tablespoon Grand Marnier (optional)

Serves 8

❶ Lightly oil the bottom and sides of a 9-inch pie plate. With a fork, mix the crumbs with the melted butter until evenly moistened. Sprinkle evenly over the bottom of the pie plate, then press firmly into place. Freeze at least 30 minutes.

❷ Meanwhile, thaw the chocolate ice cream in a large bowl until it is soft enough to spread. With a rubber spatula, spread the ice cream over the frozen crust and smooth the top. Freeze at least 1 hour.

❸ To make the truffle layer, combine the chocolate chips and cream in a saucepan over medium heat. Stir until the chocolate begins to melt, then remove from the heat and stir until very smooth. Spread evenly over the frozen pie. Freeze for 30 minutes, or until firm.

❹ Soften the vanilla ice cream in a large bowl. Spread it over the pie, then sprinkle on the walnuts. Freeze at least 1 hour, or covered up to 2 weeks.

❺ To make the raspberry sauce, place the thawed raspberries and their juice in the blender. Puree until smooth. Press through a strainer, discard the seeds, and stir in the Grand Marnier.

❻ Serve the pie in small wedges with raspberry sauce poured over each portion. Cut the pie by dipping a knife in hot water.

TOASTED ALMOND MOCHA
ICE CREAM TORTE

This is the kind of dessert culinary memories are made of. It's rich, has an incredible marriage of flavors, and it looks striking. Although this torte is of formidable size, don't be dissuaded from making it even if there are only two people in your household. It keeps well and will be just as good one to two weeks later.

1 cup chocolate wafer crumbs (about 20 wafers; *see Note*)

4 tablespoons unsalted butter, melted

3 pints coffee ice cream

1 cup whole, unblanched almonds

3 pints vanilla ice cream

½ teaspoon almond extract

MOCHA SAUCE

1 cup firmly packed light brown sugar

½ cup light corn syrup

1½ tablespoons instant coffee powder

⅔ cup heavy cream

3 ounces (3 squares) unsweetened baking chocolate, coarsely chopped

2½ tablespoons coffee liqueur

Dash salt

Serves 8

❶ Lightly oil the sides and bottom of an 8- or 9-inch springform pan. In a small bowl, combine the cookie crumbs and melted butter with a fork. Sprinkle them on the bottom of the pan, and press them in to form a bottom crust. Freeze at least 30 minutes.

❷ Soften the coffee ice cream just until you can spread it evenly on the crust. Freeze 30 minutes, or until firm.

❸ Meanwhile, roughly chop ½ cup of the almonds. Place the other ½ cup in a blender or food processor and grind to a fine powder. Combine with the chopped almonds in a pie tin or other shallow ovenproof dish and toast in a 350°F oven until fragrant and golden, 7 to 8 minutes. (Stir occasionally to prevent uneven toasting.) Let cool. Set aside 1 tablespoon of the toasted almonds.

❹ Soften the vanilla ice cream and stir in the toasted almonds and the almond extract. Spread over the coffee ice cream and smooth the top. Sprinkle on the reserved 1 tablespoon of the almonds. Cover with foil or plastic wrap and freeze 2 hours, or overnight.

(continued)

❺ To make the sauce: In a medium saucepan, combine the brown sugar, corn syrup, instant coffee, and heavy cream. Bring to a boil over medium heat, stirring constantly, and boil 5 minutes. Remove the pan from the heat. Stir in the chocolate until melted, then stir in the coffee liqueur and the salt. Keep warm or at room temperature; the sauce will thicken as it cools. (If chilled, reheat the sauce in a bowl of hot tap water and stir until of pouring consistency. Store leftover sauce in the refrigerator up to 2 weeks in a jar with a screw-on cap).

❻ Just before serving, wrap a warm, dampened kitchen towel around the sides of the springform pan and remove the rim. With a large knife dipped in hot water, cut the torte into wedges. Serve with the mocha sauce.

☞ ***Note:*** The best wafers for making a crumb crust are a plain variety such as Nabisco's Famous Chocolate Wafers. Place wafers in a plastic bag, seal, and crush with a rolling pin.

ORANGE POPPY SEED CAKE

A rich, buttery cake drizzled with a creamy white glaze — simple, yet utterly seductive. I bake this in a bundt pan because it looks so impressive, but any tube pan will do.

3 cups unbleached flour

1½ teaspoons baking powder

1½ teaspoons baking soda

¾ teaspoon salt

3 tablespoons poppy seeds

1 cup (2 sticks) unsalted butter, softened

1½ cups sugar

3 large eggs

1½ cups sour cream *or* plain yogurt

1 tablespoon pure orange extract *(see Note)*

GLAZE

1 cup confectioners' sugar

1 tablespoon warm water

½ teaspoon pure orange extract

Serves 12 to 16

❶ Preheat the oven to 350°F. Butter and flour a bundt pan or other 10-cup tube pan.

❷ In a medium bowl, thoroughly combine the flour, baking powder, baking soda, salt, and poppy seeds.

❸ In a large mixing bowl, cream together the butter and sugar with an electric mixer until light and fluffy. Beat in the eggs until mixed, then beat in the sour cream and orange extract.

❹ Beat in the flour mixture until combined, scraping the sides of the bowl as necessary. Scrape the batter into the prepared pan. Bake 50 to 55 minutes, or until a cake tester inserted in the center of the cake comes out dry. Cool 10 minutes on a wire rack before turning out. Cool completely before making the glaze.

❺ To make the glaze: Combine the confectioners' sugar, water, and orange extract in a small bowl. With a spoon, drizzle the glaze over the top of the cake. Let harden before serving, about 20 minutes.

☛*Note:* This cake freezes very well. Wrap in plastic, and cover again with foil or seal in a plastic bag. Orange extract can be purchased in most supermarkets. If necessary, you could substitute 1½ tablespoons grated orange rind and 1 tablespoon orange juice in the cake, and omit the orange extract in the glaze.

FRESH APPLE CAKE

ere is a very different apple-filled cake — the best one I know. It will still be moist and fresh-tasting 5 days after baking if well wrapped and refrigerated.

CAKE

5 medium apples, peeled, cored, and thinly sliced

1½ cups plus 2 tablespoons sugar

2 teaspoons cinnamon

3 large eggs

¾ cup vegetable oil

¼ cup plus 2 tablespoons orange juice

2¼ cups unbleached flour

2¼ teaspoons baking powder

2 teaspoons vanilla extract

GLAZE

½ cup apricot preserves

1½ tablespoons water

. . . .

2 tablespoons sliced almonds

. . . .

Sweetened whipped cream (optional)

Serves 10 to 12

❶ Preheat the oven to 350°F. Butter and flour a 9-inch tube pan.

❷ Place the apple slices in a medium bowl. Sprinkle on 2 tablespoons of the sugar and the cinnamon, and toss very well to coat. Set aside.

❸ In a large bowl, beat the eggs with an electric mixer. Add the remaining 1½ cups sugar and beat until pale and creamy. Beat in the remaining cake ingredients until well blended.

❹ Pour one-third of the batter into the prepared pan, give the apple mixture a quick toss, and spread half the apples on top of the batter. Pour on half the remaining batter (don't worry if the apples aren't completely covered), and top with the remaining apples. Pour on the remaining batter and spread to cover the apples as best you can.

❺ Bake 60 to 70 minutes, or until a knife inserted in the center of the cake comes out clean. Cool on a wire rack 10 minutes, invert onto a plate, and invert again onto a serving plate to cool right side up.

❻ To make the glaze: Heat the apricot preserves and water together until the mixture is very hot. Pour through a strainer, pressing the solid pieces through. With a pastry brush, coat the entire cake with the glaze. Sprinkle the sliced almonds on top. Let the cake cool thoroughly before serving plain or with sweetened whipped cream.

OATMEAL CAKE WITH PENUCHE FROSTING

The idea of oats in a cake may sound unusual, but in fact this buttery, light cake is one of the most delicious I've tasted. Be sure to include the cardamom, for the flavor marries superbly with the oats and brown sugar.

8 tablespoons (1 stick) unsalted butter, softened

1 cup sugar

2 large eggs, room temperature

1 teaspoon vanilla extract

1½ cups unbleached flour

1 cup oats, ground fine in a blender

3 teaspoons baking powder

1 teaspoon ground cardamom

½ teaspoon salt

1 cup milk

PENUCHE FROSTING

6 tablespoons unsalted butter

½ cup packed light brown sugar

1½ tablespoons milk

1 cup confectioners' sugar

½ teaspoon vanilla extract

. . . .

⅓ cup very finely ground pecans *or* walnuts

Serves 8

❶ Preheat the oven to 350°F. Butter and flour a 9-inch springform cake pan, or use an 8 × 8-inch square cake pan. (If your pan is made of glass, set the oven at 325°F.)

❷ In a large mixing bowl, cream the butter with an electric mixer until soft. Add the sugar and beat until well blended. Add the eggs and vanilla and beat again until light and creamy.

❸ Thoroughly combine the flour, ground oats, baking powder, cardamom, and salt in a medium bowl. Beat these ingredients into the butter mixture, alternating with the milk, until well blended. Scrape into the prepared pan and smooth the top. Bake 50 to 55 minutes, or until a knife inserted in the center of the cake comes out clean. Cool on a wire rack 15 minutes, then loosen the edges of the cake, invert onto a platter, and invert again onto the rack so the cake is right side up. Let the cake cool completely, about 2 hours.

❹ When the cake is cool, make the frosting: In a small saucepan, melt the butter over medium-low heat. Add the brown sugar and stir until melted and blended with the butter. Slowly pour in the milk, mix well, and bring the mixture to a boil. Scrape it into a medium bowl and cool 10 minutes. Add the

(continued)

confectioners' sugar and vanilla and beat with an electric mixer until smooth. Spread all over the cooled cake. Decorate the cake by sprinkling the ground nuts on top, leaving a ¾ inch border bare. Wait at least 15 minutes before serving, to allow the frosting to set.

OLD-FASHIONED POUND CAKE

This cake is great to have on hand because it's so popular and versatile. Freeze a portion to serve at a moment's notice — plain, with sliced fresh fruit, or with Strawberry and Peach Compote (page 225). Try varying the flavor by following any of the suggestions below.

1 cup (2 sticks) unsalted butter, softened

2 cups sugar

5 large eggs

2 teaspoons vanilla extract

2 cups cake flour *(see Note)*

½ teaspoon salt

Serves 10 to 12

❶ Preheat the oven to 325°F. Butter and flour a 9 × 5-inch loaf pan. In a large mixing bowl, cream the butter until smooth, using an electric mixer. Add the sugar and beat until light. Add the eggs one at a time, beating well after each addition. Beat in the vanilla extract.

❷ Add the flour and salt and beat until the batter is very smooth. Scrape the batter into the prepared pan and bake 1½ hours, or until a knife inserted in the center of the cake comes out clean. (If the cake begins to get dark before it has finished cooking, lay a sheet of foil over it during the last 15 minutes or so.) Cool on a wire rack 10 minutes before removing from the pan. Cool completely (at least 2 hours) before serving.

☛*Note:* If you don't have cake flour, substitute 1¾ cups unbleached white and ¼ cup cornstarch.

☛*Variations:* For Lemon Pound Cake, use 1 teaspoon vanilla extract, plus the grated rind of 1 lemon. For Almond Pound Cake, use ½ teaspoon vanilla extract plus ½ teaspoon almond extract. For Orange Pound Cake, use ½ teaspoon vanilla extract plus the grated rind of 1 orange or 1 teaspoon pure orange extract.

POACHED PEARS
IN GINGER SYRUP

These succulent sweet-and-spicy pears are the perfect finale for a rich meal.

2 cups water

⅔ cup sugar

7 quarter-size slices fresh ginger

4 firm ripe pears, peeled, halved, and cored

Serves 4

❶ In a large stockpot, combine the water, sugar, and ginger. Bring to a boil and stir until the sugar dissolves, about 2 minutes.

❷ Add the pears and reduce the heat to a lively simmer. Cook, basting occasionally, 15 minutes. Remove from the heat and let the pears cool in the syrup 30 minutes.

❸ With a slotted spoon, remove the pears from the liquid and place them in a bowl. Boil the syrup briskly 2 minutes, or until it thickens slightly. Pour it through a strainer onto the pears. Discard the ginger. Chill the fruit in its syrup until cold, about 2 hours. Serve in pretty bowls.

BLUEBERRY KUCHEN

Kuchen (pronounced koo'-kin) is a type of low coffee cake topped with fruit. Here, blueberries cover an almond-flavored cake that has a cookielike texture. Great for dessert, for teatime, or to pack on a picnic and eat with your fingers.

8 tablespoons (1 stick) unsalted butter, softened

⅔ cup sugar

1 large egg

1 teaspoon vanilla extract

½ teaspoon almond extract

1¼ cups unbleached flour

½ teaspoon baking powder

¼ teaspoon salt

2 cups fresh blueberries

1 tablespoon sugar

¼ teaspoon cinnamon

Serves 8

❶ In a large bowl, cream the butter with the sugar until blended. Beat in the egg, vanilla, and almond extract until pale and creamy.

❷ Add the flour, baking powder, and salt and beat until well mixed. Don't overwork the batter. Chill 30 minutes, or until the batter is no longer wet and sticky. Meanwhile, preheat the oven to 350°F. Butter a 9- or 10-inch tart pan with a removable rim.

❸ Press the batter into the bottom and sides of the tart pan. Mix the blueberries with the 1 tablespoon sugar and the cinnamon. Fill the tart shell. Bake 40 minutes, or until the cake is a rich golden brown. Cool 5 minutes on a wire rack, then place the tart pan on an inverted bowl and pull down the rim. Return the pan to the rack and cool completely before serving, about 1½ hours.

☞*Note:* This kuchen freezes exceptionally well when wrapped well in foil and sealed in a plastic bag. Thaw at room temperature a few hours before serving.

APPLE WALNUT KUCHEN

This kuchen has a buttery crust and is topped with cinnamon-coated apple slices arranged in concentric circles. Very delicious and attractive. It's rich, so small slices suffice.

8 tablespoons (1 stick) unsalted butter, softened

⅔ cup plus 1½ teaspoons sugar

1 large egg yolk

1 teaspoon vanilla extract

1 cup unbleached flour

¼ teaspoon salt

1 tablespoon milk

¼ cup finely chopped walnuts

3 large apples (not Delicious), peeled, cored, and very thinly sliced

2 tablespoons unsalted butter, melted

½ teaspoon cinnamon

Serves 8

❶ Cream the butter and the ⅔ cup sugar together in a large bowl until it is well mixed. Add the egg yolk and vanilla extract and beat until blended. Sprinkle in the flour and salt and beat just until evenly mixed. Pour in the milk and beat just until the dough begins to clump together. Chill 15 minutes.

❷ Generously butter an 8- or 9-inch tart pan with a removable rim. Pat the dough into the bottom and sides of the tart pan. Chill 30 minutes.

❸ Preheat the oven to 350°F. Sprinkle the walnuts evenly over the bottom of the crust. Place the apple slices in the crust in concentric circles; you probably will have 2 layers. Brush the top layer with the melted butter.

❹ Mix the remaining 1½ teaspoons sugar with the cinnamon and sprinkle evenly over the apples. Bake 40 minutes, or until the crust is a rich golden brown and the apples are tender. Cool on a wire rack 10 minutes, then remove the rim of the tart pan. Cool completely before serving.

THE BEST
CHOCOLATE CAKE

*M*any arrogant cooks
think they have the best chocolate cake recipe.
They're all wrong; I have it!
   The basis of this recipe is what is known as a
wacky cake: such a cake has no eggs, and everything is quickly mixed in one bowl. For some
marvelous reason, it creates an ultramoist, rich,
memorable two-layer cake, which I frost with
the silkiest chocolate buttercream icing you've
ever tasted.

CAKE

2¼ cups unbleached white
flour

1½ cups sugar

½ cup cocoa

1½ teaspoons baking soda

¾ teaspoon salt

1½ cups warm water

½ cup vegetable oil

1½ teaspoons vanilla extract

1½ teaspoons white vinegar

ICING

1 cup semisweet chocolate
chips

8 tablespoons (1 stick)
unsalted butter, softened

1 large egg

Serves 8

❶ Preheat the oven to 350°F. Wait 10 minutes before starting to make the cake. Meanwhile, butter and flour 2 8-inch layer pans and set aside. When the 10 minutes are up, thoroughly combine the flour, sugar, cocoa, baking soda, and salt in a bowl.

❷ Pour in the water, oil, vanilla, and vinegar and stir until well combined. Pour into the prepared pans. Bake 30 minutes, or until a knife inserted in the center of the cake comes out clean. Cool on a wire rack 10 minutes, then remove the cakes from the pans and cool completely.

❸ To make the buttercream: Melt the chocolate in a double boiler, then remove the top pan. Let the chocolate cool until tepid. In a medium bowl, cream the butter, using an electric mixer. Add the egg and beat until blended but not smooth. Pour in the chocolate and beat just until combined.

❹ When the cake is completely cool, spread some icing on one layer. Top with the other layer, then spread the remaining icing all over the cake. Chill the cake at least 30 minutes, then bring to room temperature before serving.

DEEP-DISH PEAR PIE

A thick and flaky clove-scented crust covers succulent pears bathed in their own juices. A splendid dessert for fruit lovers.

6 ripe Bosc, Anjou, or Comice pears

½ cup sugar

1 tablespoon fresh lemon juice

1 teaspoon pure vanilla extract

2 tablespoons cornstarch

CRUST

1 cup unbleached flour

¼ teaspoon ground cloves

Dash salt

5 tablespoons cold unsalted butter

1 tablespoon vegetable oil

2 tablespoons water

1 large egg, beaten

Serves 4 to 6

❶ Preheat the oven to 425°F. Peel and core the pears and slice them into bite-size pieces. Drop them into a 1½-quart baking dish and mix in the sugar, lemon juice, vanilla extract, and cornstarch.

❷ To make the crust: Mix the flour, cloves, and salt in a medium bowl. Cut the butter into small bits and work it into the flour with your fingers or a pastry cutter until it resembles coarse meal. Pour on the oil, stir, and sprinkle on the water. Work the mixture until you can gather it in a ball, then knead the dough 2 or 3 times to blend.

❸ Roll the dough on a floured surface into a circle large enough to cover the pear mixture. Drape it over the pears, cut a vent in the center, and brush the crust with the beaten egg.

❹ Bake 10 minutes, then reduce the heat to 350°F. Cook 40 minutes longer, or until the crust is a nice golden brown. Cool on a rack and serve warm.

FRESH STRAWBERRY TART

*This glorious tart is
rather quick to assemble because you don't have
to roll out the crust or cook the filling. Other
summer fruit works well; try blueberries, raspberries, peaches, or plums.*

ALMOND CRUST

5 tablespoons unsalted
butter, softened

1 large egg yolk

½ teaspoon vanilla extract

3 tablespoons sugar

⅔ cup almonds

1 cup unbleached flour

FILLING

8 ounces Neufchâtel or
cream cheese, at room
temperature

¼ cup sugar

2 tablespoons fresh lemon
juice

¼ cup heavy cream

1 to 1½ pints fresh
strawberries, hulled

¼ cup apricot preserves

1 tablespoon water

Serves 6

❶ Preheat the oven to 350°F. Butter the sides of a
9- to 10-inch tart pan with a removable rim or set
aside a 9-inch pie plate.

❷ To make the crust: In a large bowl, beat the butter, egg yolk, vanilla, and sugar until smooth and
creamy. Finely grind the almonds, then combine
with the flour and beat in just until mixed. The
dough will be crumbly; don't overwork. Gather the
dough into a ball, then break off pieces and press it
into the bottom and sides of the tart pan or pie
plate. Prick the crust all over with a fork. Chill
1 hour, or cover and freeze for up to 2 weeks.

❸ Line the crust with foil, then cover the bottom
with dried beans or pie weights. Bake 12 minutes.
Remove the foil and beans and bake 10 minutes
longer, or until golden all over. Cool completely on a
wire rack. If using a tart pan, remove the outer rim.

❹ To make the filling: Beat the cream cheese, sugar,
and lemon juice together. Pour in the cream and beat
until very smooth. Spread on the bottom of the tart.

❺ Cover the tart with strawberries in a decorative
manner. Heat the preserves and water together
until blended. Strain out any bits of pulp through a
mesh strainer. Brush the glaze on the strawberries
with a pastry brush. Chill the tart 4 hours, or overnight, before serving. Serve cool, not cold.

CRANBERRIES. Oftentimes grocery stores abound with bags of cranberries around the Thanksgiving holiday, and then the berries mysteriously disappear for the remaining eleven months of the year. To overcome this frustration, I always purchase a few extra bags and keep them in the freezer. Cranberries freeze exceptionally well, retaining their shape and firm texture.

When I want to use cranberries in a recipe, I take out the amount needed, rinse the cranberries in a strainer under cold running water to remove any pesticides, and pat them dry before incorporating them in a recipe.

MAPLE FRUIT CRISP

*M aple syrup sweetens
this winter fruit dessert. It's great for conquering
the winter doldrums.*

5 medium apples (any type
but Delicious), peeled,
cored, and thinly sliced

2 firm ripe Anjou, Comice,
or Bartlett pears, peeled,
cored, and thinly sliced

⅔ cup fresh or frozen
cranberries

2 tablespoons golden raisins

3 tablespoons pure maple
syrup

1 tablespoon unbleached
flour

TOPPING

¼ cup unbleached flour

¼ cup oats

2 tablespoons finely
chopped walnuts

¼ cup firmly packed light
brown sugar

1 teaspoon ground
cinnamon

¼ teaspoon salt

5 tablespoons cold unsalted
butter, cut into bits

3 tablespoons pure maple
syrup

Serves 4 to 6

❶ Preheat the oven to 350°F. In a large bowl, combine the apples, pears, cranberries, raisins, and maple syrup. Toss to coat well. Sprinkle on the flour and toss again. Scrape the fruit into an 8 × 8-inch pan and smooth the top.

❷ To make the topping: Combine the flour, oats, walnuts, brown sugar, cinnamon, and salt in a medium bowl. With your fingertips, rub in the butter bits until coarse crumbs form. Stir in the maple syrup just until the crumbs are evenly moistened (the mixture will be a little gooey). With your fingers, sprinkle the mixture on top of the fruit, breaking up any large chunks.

❸ Bake 40 to 50 minutes, or until the filling is bubbly and the apples are tender. Serve warm or at room temperature.

RHUBARB CRUMBLE

The cardamom flavor is outstanding in this absolutely delicious dessert. The apples give the rhubarb filling some body, and it all turns a beautiful rosy hue.

4 cups (about 1¼ pounds) diced rhubarb

3 Granny Smith apples, peeled, cored, and thinly sliced

¾ cup honey

1½ tablespoons cornstarch

½ teaspoon ground cardamom

TOPPING

½ cup unbleached flour

½ cup firmly packed light brown sugar

½ teaspoon cinnamon

¼ teaspoon salt

5 tablespoons cold unsalted butter, cut into bits

2 tablespoons slivered almonds

Serves 6

❶ Preheat the oven to 350°F. In a large bowl, combine the rhubarb, apples, honey, cornstarch, and cardamom. Pour the fruit into an 8 × 8 × 2-inch baking pan and smooth the top.

❷ To make the topping: Combine the flour, brown sugar, cinnamon, and salt in a medium bowl. Add the butter bits and stir to coat. With your fingertips, rub the butter into the mixture until coarse crumbs form. Stir in the almonds. Sprinkle the crumbs all over the top of the rhubarb filling.

❸ Bake 50 minutes, or until the topping is brown and the filling is bubbly. Serve slightly warm or at room temperature.

FRUIT COUPE

This is a very pretty, light dessert. It's worthwhile investing in some decorative dessert goblets so that with a dessert such as this you can make a stunning presentation with little effort. Below is my favorite combination of fruit. Feel free to improvise as desired.

⅔ cup heavy cream, well chilled

1½ tablespoons confectioners' sugar

¼ teaspoon almond extract

1½ cups fresh blueberries

2 peaches, peeled and sliced

1 ripe banana, cut into ½-inch slices

1 tablespoon sliced almonds, lightly toasted

Serves 4

❶ Whip the cream with the sugar and almond extract until stiff. (This can be done up to 2 hours in advance and the whipped cream refrigerated.)

❷ Set 4 decorative goblets in front of you. Using half the fruit, divide it evenly among the goblets. Spoon on half the whipped cream. Top with the remaining fruit, then with the remaining whipped cream. Sprinkle some almonds on each portion. Serve immediately.

PEACH MELBA

Each summer my family eagerly awaits raspberry season so we can savor this memorable dessert. Many people poach fresh peaches in sugar syrup when they make Peach Melba, but I find this step unnecessary with really ripe, sweet, juicy peaches. I think this dessert looks stunning in pretty dessert goblets that show off its striking colors, but small dessert dishes will do.

1⅔ cups fresh raspberries

3 tablespoons plus
2 teaspoons sugar

½ cup heavy cream, chilled

2 ripe peaches

1⅓ pints rich vanilla ice cream

12 whole raspberries, for garnish

Serves 4

❶ Put the raspberries in a blender or food processor and puree until smooth. Strain through a medium-mesh strainer into a small bowl and press out all the juice from the pulp. Discard the seeds. (Alternatively, lay a piece of cheesecloth over a medium bowl so that it hangs over the edges, and pour a small amount of the puree into it. Gather up the sides and gently squeeze out the juice. Discard the seeds and repeat with the rest of the puree.) Stir 2 tablespoons plus 2 teaspoons of the sugar into the sauce, cover, and chill at least 2 hours.

❷ Whip the cream (it is a good idea to chill the bowl and beaters beforehand) until it begins to thicken, then sprinkle on the remaining 1 tablespoon of the sugar and whip until stiff. Cover and chill until ready to use.

❸ To assemble: Peel the peaches, cut them in half lengthwise, and discard the stone. Scoop ¼ of the ice cream into each dish, then gently press a peach half—cut side down—into the ice cream. Spoon on equal portions of the raspberry sauce. Top with the whipped cream (I like to use a pastry bag and pipe the cream using a star tip). Decorate each serving with 3 whole raspberries.

FRESH BLUEBERRIES WITH STRAWBERRY CREAM

*S*trawberry jam gives
whipped cream a pink caste that contrasts beautifully with blueberries layered in goblets.

1 pint fresh blueberries

3 tablespoons strawberry
jam

⅔ cup heavy cream, well
chilled

Serves 4

❶ Rinse the blueberries in a colander and drain very well. Pick out and discard any blemished berries.

❷ Place the jam in a large mixing bowl and beat a few seconds with an electric mixer. Pour in the heavy cream and whip until stiff.

❸ In attractive goblets, layer the blueberries with the strawberry cream, making 3 layers of blueberries and two layers of cream. Chill until ready to serve, but no longer than 2 hours.

EGGNOG DIP FOR FRUIT

ere is a very different idea given me by my friend Billie Chernicoff: an eggnog-flavored dessert dip for fresh fruit. I've taken a rich, rum-and-nutmeg-spiked pastry cream and folded whipped cream into it.

Serve the dip in a beautiful bowl surrounded with a striking assortment of fruit that includes strawberries; banana, apple, and pear slices; and an attractively carved pineapple.

3 large egg yolks

⅓ cup plus 1 tablespoon sugar

1½ tablespoons cornstarch

2 tablespoons plus 1 teaspoon rum

⅛ teaspoon freshly grated nutmeg

1½ cups milk

½ teaspoon vanilla extract

½ cup heavy cream, well chilled

1 strawberry, for garnish

Serves 8

❶ In a large bowl, whisk the egg yolks and sugar until well blended. Whisk in the cornstarch until smooth, then whisk in 2 tablespoons of the rum and the nutmeg. Place a medium bowl on the counter for use in Step 3.

❷ Heat the milk in a medium saucepan over medium-high heat until very hot but not boiling. Slowly whisk the milk into the egg yolk mixture, then return the mixture to the saucepan. Whisking constantly, bring the mixture to a boil. Boil 1 minute, or until thickened like a custard.

❸ With a rubber spatula, immediately scrape the custard into the reserved bowl. Whisk in the vanilla. (If for some reason the custard is not smooth, pour it through a strainer.) Cover with plastic wrap, pressing it directly onto the custard to prevent a skin from forming. Chill until cold, at least 2 hours and up to 24 hours.

❹ No more than 4 hours before serving, whip the cream until very stiff. Gently but thoroughly fold it into the custard, along with the remaining 1 teaspoon rum. Scrape the dip into a serving bowl and garnish with the strawberry. Chill until serving time.

STRAWBERRY AND PEACH COMPOTE

*S*trawberries and
*peaches swim in a heavenly wine-flavored syrup
that accentuates their flavors. Because the alcohol
is boiled away, this dessert is suitable for children
and is always popular with them.*

¾ cup water

¾ cup dry white or red wine

½ cup sugar

2 cups fresh strawberries,
hulled and halved

4 fresh peaches (about
2 cups), peeled and sliced

Serves 4 to 6

❶ In a small saucepan, combine the water, wine, and sugar and bring to a boil. Boil 30 seconds. Refrigerate until cold, about 1 hour.

❷ Combine the strawberries and peaches in a bowl and pour the syrup over them. Chill 4 to 12 hours. Serve cold in decorative goblets with a sprig of fresh mint.

GLAZED CARDAMOM PEARS

Juicy, sweet pears don't need much embellishment. These are baked with a brown sugar–cardamom syrup and served with sweetened sour cream.

1½ tablespoons unsalted butter

2 tablespoons firmly packed light brown sugar

2 ripe pears, peeled, halved, and cored

½ teaspoon ground cardamom

¼ cup water

¼ cup sour cream

2 teaspoons firmly packed light brown sugar

Serves 2

❶ Preheat the oven to 400°F. Grease the bottom of a 9-inch pie plate or shallow baking dish with 1 tablespoon of the butter and sprinkle on 1 tablespoon of the brown sugar. Place the pears in the dish cut side down, and sprinkle on the cardamom and the remaining 1 tablespoon brown sugar. Pour the water into the dish. Bake 30 minutes, turning the pears twice.

❷ Meanwhile, mix the sour cream with the brown sugar and chill until ready to serve.

❸ Serve the pears warm or at room temperature, with any remaining syrup drizzled over them. Top each serving with a few spoonfuls of the sweetened sour cream.

COFFEE MOUSSE

Coffee lovers take note!
This silken mousse layered with bits of semisweet
chocolate makes a rich but delicate finale for a
special meal.

1 cup strong coffee

1 cup milk

4 large egg yolks

½ cup plus 2 tablespoons sugar

3 tablespoons cornstarch

½ tablespoon unsalted butter, melted

½ cup heavy cream, well chilled

4 teaspoons minced semisweet chocolate

Serves 4 to 6

❶ Combine the coffee and milk in a heavy saucepan and heat until hot but not boiling.

❷ Meanwhile, place the egg yolks, ½ cup of the sugar, and the cornstarch in a large bowl and whisk until pale and creamy.

❸ Slowly whisk the hot milk into the egg mixture until blended, and return to the saucepan, setting aside the bowl. Whisking constantly, bring the mixture to a boil. Boil 1 minute, whisking often. Pour into the bowl, then whisk in the butter. Cover by placing plastic wrap directly on the custard to prevent a skin from forming. Refrigerate until cold, about 2 hours.

❹ The custard will now be firm, so whisk gently to smooth and lighten it. Whip the cream with the remaining 2 tablespoons sugar until stiff but not buttery. With a rubber spatula, fold the cream into the custard until evenly incorporated.

❺ Spoon half the mousse into 4 8-ounce dessert goblets (or 6 smaller goblets). Divide half the minced chocolate among the portions. Spoon the remaining mousse on top of the chocolate, and sprinkle the remaining chocolate on top of each portion. Chill 30 minutes before serving. Cover each dish with plastic wrap if chilling longer. These can be stored in the refrigerator for up to 24 hours.

ALMOND RICE PUDDING

I've experimented with many versions of rice pudding in order to develop the perfect one — easy to prepare, very creamy, and unusually delicious. I think you'll agree that this is it.

4 cups low-fat milk, scalded

½ cup converted white rice

½ cup plus 3 tablespoons sugar

1 cinnamon stick

½ teaspoon salt

2 large egg yolks

½ cup milk

½ cup raisins

1 teaspoon vanilla extract

¼ teaspoon almond extract

⅔ cup heavy cream, well chilled

Sliced almonds, for garnish

Serves 6 generously

❶ Bring water to a boil in the bottom of a double boiler. In the top, combine the scalded milk, rice, ½ cup of the sugar, the cinnamon stick, and the salt. Cook, covered, over medium heat 45 to 50 minutes, or until the rice is tender. Stir occasionally to prevent sticking.

❷ In a medium bowl, whisk together the egg yolks and the ½ cup milk. Ladle in some of the hot rice mixture, stir, and carefully pour the yolk mixture into the pudding. Stir to blend. Cover and cook 10 minutes, stirring occasionally. Mix in the raisins and cook, covered, 20 minutes longer, or until the pudding thickens. Continue to stir periodically to prevent sticking.

❸ Remove the cinnamon stick and discard. Stir in the vanilla and almond extracts. Scrape the pudding into a large bowl, cover, and chill until cold, at least 2 hours. (It is a good idea to put your beaters in the freezer at this time.)

❹ Whip the cream until it begins to stiffen, then sprinkle in the remaining 3 tablespoons sugar and whip until stiff. Fold the cream into the cold pudding and spoon individual portions into 6 decorative goblets or dishes. Garnish with the sliced almonds. Serve immediately, or cover and chill for up to 24 hours before serving.

BREAD PUDDING WITH BOURBON SAUCE

I had this unforgettable bread pudding in New Orleans and was finally able to duplicate it in my kitchen.

PUDDING

1 8-ounce loaf day-old French or Italian bread, torn into small pieces (about 8 cups)

3 cups low-fat milk

2 large eggs, beaten

1 cup sugar

½ cup raisins

2 tablespoons vanilla extract

1 tablespoon cold unsalted butter, cut into bits

BOURBON SAUCE

6 tablespoons unsalted butter

1 large egg

¾ cup confectioners' sugar

3 tablespoons bourbon whiskey

Serves 8

❶ Butter a deep 2-quart baking dish and set aside.

❷ Tear the bread into small pieces and drop them into a large bowl. Pour the milk over them and stir to moisten. Soak 30 minutes. (About 20 minutes after beginning to soak the bread, preheat the oven to 350°F.) When finished soaking, break up the bread into bits with a large spoon.

❸ Beat together the eggs, sugar, raisins, and vanilla. Pour into the bread mixture and stir thoroughly, breaking up any large chunks of bread that surface. Scrape the pudding into the prepared baking dish, smooth the top, and dot with the butter. Place the baking dish in a large pan and fill the outer pan halfway with hot water. Place both pans in the oven and bake 70 minutes, or until a knife inserted in the center of the pudding comes out clean.

❹ Meanwhile, make the sauce: Melt the butter in a double boiler. In a small bowl, beat the egg, and beat in the confectioners' sugar. Stir into the melted butter, and whisk the mixture until it becomes very hot, about 7 minutes. Do not boil. Remove from the heat and scrape into a bowl. Let cool to room temperature, stirring occasionally. The sauce will thicken as it cools. Stir in the bourbon.

❺ Serve the pudding hot or warm in small custard cups. Spoon some sauce over each serving.

SWEET POTATO PUDDING WITH CRYSTALLIZED GINGER

This nutritious, spicy pudding is cooked in individual custard or soufflé cups, inverted, and topped with whipped cream and crystallized ginger. If you cannot get crystallized ginger, preserved ginger in syrup can be substituted. Try to get yams for their bright color, although regular sweet potatoes will still be delicious.

3 medium-large (about 1¼ pounds) yams or sweet potatoes

1¼ cups low-fat milk

¾ cup pure maple syrup, *or* ⅔ cup honey

3 large eggs

¼ cup unbleached flour

2 teaspoons cinnamon

1 teaspoon ground allspice

¼ teaspoon salt

2 tablespoons finely chopped crystallized ginger, plus 2 teaspoons, for garnish *(see Note)*

Lightly sweetened whipped cream

Serves 8

❶ Butter 8 ¾-cup custard cups or small soufflé dishes and set aside.

❷ Scrub the sweet potatoes, and cut each in half. Bring a medium saucepan of water to a boil, and cook the sweet potatoes until very tender, about 25 minutes. About 10 minutes before the sweet potatoes are done, preheat the oven to 350°F.

❸ Drain the sweet potatoes thoroughly. When cool enough to handle, peel off the skins and mash the flesh. Measure out 2¼ cups mashed sweet potato. (Any remaining sweet potato can be reheated and served with butter.)

❹ Put the mashed sweet potato, milk, maple syrup or honey, eggs, flour, cinnamon, allspice, and salt in a blender or food processor and blend until very smooth. Turn off the processor and stir in the 2 tablespoons crystallized ginger by hand.

❺ Pour the mixture into the prepared custard cups (it's OK to fill them almost to the tops). Place the cups in a large pan, and fill the outside pan with enough hot water to reach halfway up the sides of the cups.

❻ Bake 1 hour, or until the pudding pulls away from the sides of the cups and a knife inserted in the center of the pudding comes out almost clean. Remove the cups from the water bath, and cool on a wire rack at least 20 minutes, but no longer than 45 minutes. Run a knife around the edge of each pudding, and invert onto individual small plates or a large platter. Serve at room temperature, or chilled slightly, with spoonfuls of whipped cream and a few pieces of chopped crystallized ginger topping the cream.

☞*Note:* Crystallized ginger can be purchased in most specialty food shops and in many supermarkets, often in the Chinese-food section.

MENUS

An asterisk indicates a
recipe not given in the text.

EASY DINNERS

MIXED GREEN SALAD WITH ARUGULA * AND
BLUE CHEESE VINAIGRETTE

CAPELLINI WITH TOMATO PESTO

FRENCH BREAD *

POACHED PEARS IN GINGER SYRUP

SPICY MIXED NUTS

VEGETABLE CURRY

BASMATI RICE *

WARM PITA BREAD *

OATMEAL CAKE WITH PENUCHE FROSTING

MIXED GREEN SALAD OF BOSTON LETTUCE AND
WATERCRESS * WITH DOUBLE SESAME DRESSING

ZUCCHINI, TOMATO, AND SWISS CHEESE PIE

BULGHUR MUSHROOM PILAF

FRUIT COUPE

CRUDITÉS * WITH CREAMY CURRY DIP

MUSHROOM PIE

COUSCOUS PILAF WITH PEAS

COFFEE MOUSSE

GREEN SALAD * WITH TAHINI SALAD DRESSING

PASTA AND VEGETABLE GRATIN

GARLIC BREAD *

MAPLE FRUIT CRISP

MIXED GREEN SALAD * WITH CREAMY HERB VINAIGRETTE

RAVIOLI WITH GARLIC, PEPPERS, AND TOMATOES

FRENCH BREAD *

ALMOND RICE PUDDING

MARINATED ROASTED PEPPERS ON FRENCH BREAD TOASTS

CHILAQUILES

STEAMED GREEN BEANS *

THE BEST CHOCOLATE CAKE

CRUDITÉS * WITH SPICY PEANUT DIP

SPICY STIR-FRIED TOFU, PEPPERS, AND MANDARIN
ORANGES

RICE *

OLD-FASHIONED POUND CAKE

OLIVADA WITH FRENCH BREAD TOASTS

SPICY RAGOUT OF VEGETABLES AND TOFU

BROWN RICE WITH OLIVE OIL AND PARMESAN CHEESE *

BREAD PUDDING WITH BOURBON SAUCE

JALAPEÑO CHEESE NACHOS

BAKED STUFFED TOMATOES WITH COUSCOUS,
PEAS, AND FETA CHEESE

STEAMED GREEN BEANS *

FRENCH BREAD *

BLUEBERRY KUCHEN

GREEN SALAD WITH ROMAINE LETTUCE, RED ONION,
AND CROUTONS * AND CREAMY GARLIC DRESSING

BARLEY MUSHROOM CASSEROLE

MASHED BUTTERNUT SQUASH *

MAPLE FRUIT CRISP

GREEN BEAN SALAD WITH LEMON, DILL, AND FETA CHEESE

BAKED COUSCOUS WITH SPINACH AND PINE NUTS

FRENCH BREAD *

OLD-FASHIONED POUND CAKE

SOUP MEALS

MIXED GREEN SALAD OF ROMAINE LETTUCE, CUCUMBERS,
GRATED CARROT, AND SCALLIONS * WITH MISO DRESSING

MUSHROOM SOUP WITH HERBS

IRISH BROWN BREAD

OATMEAL CAKE WITH PENUCHE FROSTING

GREEN BEAN SALAD WITH LEMON, DILL, AND FETA CHEESE

CORN CHOWDER

HERB OAT BREAD

DEEP-DISH PEAR PIE

JALAPEÑO CHEESE NACHOS

SPINACH SALAD WITH GRATED CARROT, MUSHROOMS,
AND RED ONION * WITH CREAMY GARLIC DRESSING

MEXICAN VEGETABLE STEW

MAPLE FRUIT CRISP

MIXED GREEN SALAD OF ROMAINE LETTUCE,
SPINACH, RED ONION, AND
SESAME SEEDS * WITH TAHINI SALAD DRESSING

CURRIED BARLEY AND MUSHROOM SOUP

RICH CREAM CHEESE BISCUITS

COFFEE MOUSSE OR POACHED PEARS IN GINGER SYRUP

BLUE CHEESE LOG

COUSCOUS AND VEGETABLE SALAD WITH ORANGE
AND GARLIC

FRENCH BREAD *

PEACH MELBA

CRUDITÉS * WITH SPICY PEANUT DIP

COLD SZECHUAN NOODLES WITH SHREDDED VEGETABLES

CRISPY GARLIC TOASTS

ALMOND RICE PUDDING

CHÈVRE TOASTS WITH ASSORTED TOPPINGS

WILD RICE SALAD WITH APPLES AND WALNUTS

RUSSIAN-STYLE MARINATED MUSHROOMS

ICE CREAM TRUFFLE PIE WITH RASPBERRY SAUCE
OR STRAWBERRY AND PEACH COMPOTE

CHILLED AVOCADO SOUP

TORTELLINI SALAD PRIMAVERA

FRENCH BREAD *

TOASTED ALMOND MOCHA ICE CREAM TORTE
OR RHUBARB CRUMBLE

EGGPLANT CAVIAR

MEDITERRANEAN PASTA SALAD WITH CHICK-PEAS
AND ROASTED PEPPERS

FRESH STRAWBERRY TART

VEGETARIAN BARBECUES

CORN-ON-THE-COB WITH CHILI-GARLIC BUTTER

TEMPEH TERIYAKI SHISH KEBAB

GRILLED MUSHROOMS

COLD ORIENTAL NOODLES WITH PEANUT SAUCE

ORANGE POPPY SEED CAKE

GRILLED CORN-ON-THE-COB

TOFU SHISH KEBAB WITH LEMON-SOY MARINADE

GRILLED EGGPLANT WITH SPICY PEANUT SAUCE

CRISPY GARLIC TOASTS

BLUEBERRY KUCHEN

APPETIZER PARTY
FOR 15 PEOPLE

STUFFED CHERRY TOMATOES (DOUBLE RECIPE)

CHEESE CRACKERS

CRISPY GARLIC TOASTS (CROSTINI)

CRUDITÉS * WITH GREEN GODDESS DIP (DOUBLE RECIPE)

STUFFED MUSHROOMS WITH SPINACH, FETA CHEESE,
AND PINE NUTS (DOUBLE RECIPE)

EGGPLANT CAVIAR

MEDITERRANEAN PASTA SALAD WITH CHICK-PEAS
AND ROASTED PEPPERS

BULGHUR SALAD WITH CORN, ZUCCHINI, AND SHREDDED BASIL

ASSORTED TEA SANDWICHES

FRESH APPLE CAKE

EGGNOG DIP WITH FRESH FRUIT

A VEGETARIAN BUFFET
FOR 10 PEOPLE

═══════

CHÈVRE TOASTS WITH ASSORTED TOPPINGS

VEGETABLE ENCHILADAS (USE 10 TORTILLAS)

BAKED STUFFED TOMATOES WITH COUSCOUS, PEAS,
AND FETA CHEESE (USE 5 MEDIUM TOMATOES)

WILD RICE SALAD WITH APPLES AND WALNUTS

PENNE AND BROCCOLI SALAD WITH CREAMY
GARLIC DRESSING

ORANGE POPPY SEED CAKE

FRUIT SALAD *

A THANKSGIVING FEAST

═══════

MOLDED WHITE BEAN PÂTÉ

SPINACH SOUP WITH SEMOLINA CHEESE DUMPLINGS

HERB OAT BREAD

MIXED GREEN SALAD OF RED-LEAF LETTUCE, WATERCRESS,
AND RED ONION * WITH DOUBLE SESAME DRESSING

WILD MUSHROOM TART IN PUFF PASTRY

COUSCOUS PILAF WITH PEAS

TOMATOES PROVENÇAL

SWEET POTATO PUDDING WITH CRYSTALLIZED
GINGER OR MAPLE FRUIT CRISP

INDEX